Introduction

Some might think it bewildering how the café racer scene has evolved to such an extent that what were at first thought of as simple, stripped-back bikes built by home-brew enthusiasts in garden sheds, has morphed into a segment where some of the leading marques in the motorcycling world stepped forward to create an astonishing sea change in skill-base, design and creativity. That created problems for prospective buyers, because suddenly the fascination in this style of bike that had become such an icon offered an over-abundance of options.

Possibly what at one time was thought of as a fad had become normality, as retro-themed models sat comfortably alongside the steady rise in popularity of scramblers and bobbers. The balloon that was expected to burst just grew bigger and better. Today, one doesn't have to push through overgrown stinging nettles and brambles to reach that torch-lit garden shed where the next-door neighbour is fettling in oily jeans. Far easier to pop along to your local Triumph or Kawasaki dealer to see what is on offer.

Back in the day, and we are talking 1950s and 60s, when most of Europe was still in recovery mode after the war, those youths with money in their pockets had their sights set on two wheels. Not just any two wheels, but those production bikes that were ripe for stripping and remodification. And while it was all about performance, said bikers were not pro-racers, experienced at racing starts and fast track days. Instead, they took inspiration from the racers of the day to build one-off machines that emulated their heroes; enthusiasts with a good eye, a sense of style, and brazen enough to not be afraid to wield a spanner.

Every decade since has witnessed modified or new variants emerging; modern twists on established marques, or new models in vintage attire, if you like. The hyphenated modern-retro is often bandied about, and that about sums it up nicely as we continue to experience exponential growth in this sector of an ever-present market.

Today's production model genre can possibly lay claim to the modern hereditary line which was inspired almost 20 years ago when Ducati revealed its Sport Classic at the 2003 Tokyo Motor Show. Revealed was one modern L-Twin clothed in vintage aesthetics. The Sport Classics were inspired by Ducati's Pierre Terblanche designed, limited-edition 2002 Mike Hailwood replica MH900e, of which only 2000 ever made it out of the factory gate due to their commercial failure. Despite the odd design fault, the bike had some neat design touches and proven performance, so if you see one come up on the open market, and you have the available cash, the retro-styled bike would well be worth adding to a collection.

With Ducati already having thrown its hat into the ring, Triumph was not far behind in the coming of the modern café racer craze with the launch of the

Thruxton. Then along [...] looking to grab a slice of the action. So, what of the shed guys and customising shops? Well, they were certainly not prepared to down tools, instead continuing to pursue their own dreams of creating the perfect café racer. Today, those same mod builders are happy to sell on their creations before returning to the drawing board with imaginations running rife.

While you will note through the following pages that many builders have stuck to traditional roots with retro-styled naked bikes with seat humps, small screens, lowered handlebars, and fairings around single headlights, not all bikes have paid homage to the aggressive riding position. In a way, while creating more speed by lessening weight and introducing better handling have been well served by tradition, there has been a noticeable movement away from the norm. Modern retro bikes may well retain the stripped-back look, but comfort is no longer taking a back seat (not that there ever was one). That's why in the following pages I am bringing to the table an eclectic mix of bikes, some you might agree with as sitting comfortably within the café racer circle, others you might not, but it is all subjective.

As I have grown older and matured in my thinking, so, too, has my take on café racers. While today's iterations retain their focus on performance but with modern upgrades, much of it comes down to looks, style, and how much you are prepared to pay. Consider, perhaps, what you can live with or live without. And that is where intended use rears its head. Exactly what are you going to use the bike for? If you want to simply fire yourself as fast as possible (and the law allows) along to the local café in a hunched-up position and with your neck cricked upwards, that's fine. But it's not very practical if you intend on using your bike for commuting or a day ride. Diversity is key, so if you are on the hunt for a new bike, consider the aesthetics and modern niceties, and explore all options available to you. One example could be that at some stage you intend to carry a passenger. No, that's not sacrilege, just common sense. You can, for example, find bikes with removable tail cowls, underneath of which lurks a passenger seat. So, my message is, don't be put off by what other people may say. Follow your instincts, as you won't go far wrong. After all, it's your money, so it's your choice.

As a footnote, I would like to take this opportunity to thank all those of you who bought the first issue of Café Racer International across the world. Your support was really appreciated, so much so that the publisher decided on a second issue. Hopefully, this one will not be the last. Meanwhile, enjoy the ride.

MICHAEL COWTON
EDITOR
MCOWTON@MORTONS.CO.UK

IMAGE: MAXINE GRUNDY

FEATURES

ON THE ROAD

MY RIDE

EDITOR/CHIEF SCRIBE:
MICHAEL COWTON

DESIGN:
GARETH WILLIAMS

PUBLISHER:
STEVE O'HARA

PUBLISHING DIRECTOR:
DAN SAVAGE

MARKETING:
TOM ASHMORE

COMMERCIAL DIRECTOR:
NIGEL HOLE

THANKS TO:
DAVE MANNING, ROSS MOWBRAY, NATASHA SWABY, ANTOINE HOTERMANS, MAXINE GRUNDY, *GETAPIC, HONDA, HARLEY-DAVIDSON, INDIAN MOTORCYCLE, NORTON, KAWASAKI, YAMAHA

***GETAPIC.CO.UK** IS A CREATIVE, FUN AND UPBEAT TEAM OF COLLABORATING PHOTOGRAPHERS, WHO TOGETHER COVER ROADSIDE PHOTOGRAPHY FOR MOTORCYCLISTS AND CAR ENTHUSIASTS, BIKER EVENTS, MOTORSPORTS, SHOWS, RALLIES AND CHARITY EVENTS ACROSS THE UNITED KINGDOM

PUBLISHED BY:
MORTONS MEDIA GROUP LTD, MEDIA CENTRE, MORTON WAY, HORNCASTLE LINCOLNSHIRE LN9 6JR

TEL: **01507 529529**

PRINTED BY: **WILLIAM GIBBONS AND SONS, WOLVERHAMPTON**

ISBN: **978-1-911639-37-4**

COVER **NORTON V4CR**

BACK COVER: **TRIUMPH THRUXTON RS TON UP SPECIAL EDITION**

MORTONS
MEDIA GROUP LTD

Independent publisher since 1885

NORTON REVEALS NEW V4 CAFÉ RACER PROTOTYPE

NORTON MOTORCYCLES RECENTLY revealed a new café racer derivative of the V4SV superbike, and it is anticipated to be one of the most powerful British café racers with its 185bhp V4 engine.

The first prototype to be designed, engineered and built at the recently opened global headquarters in the UK reintroduces fans to Norton's iconic café racer heritage and made its public debut at Motorcycle Live 2021 at Birmingham NEC.

Sharing the same engineering DNA, 185bhp 1200cc V4 engine and engineering advancements from the V4SV, the new V4CR's stripped-back appearance showcases the unrivalled craftsmanship and uncompromising quality behind one of the most powerful British café racers out there. Fitted with a carbon fibre fuel tank and body panels, polished billet aluminium swingarm and frame, the V4CR also features compact framework and a shorter rear frame for an aggressive and commanding stance.

"The prototype VC4R is the next step in Norton's strategic growth plan on its journey to becoming the world leader in luxury handcrafted motorcycles," Dr Robert Hentschel, chief executive officer of Norton Motorcycles, told *CRI*.

The V4CR prototype is Norton's latest project to use the marque's refined V4 platform, revised over the last sixteen months by a team of 30 engineers and subject to tens of thousands of road and track miles, as part of Norton's unrelenting development process.

In essence, the V4 café racer is the rebellious younger brother to the V4SV, sharing the same superbike DNA but differing in attitude and emotion. Its stripped-back fairing reveals Norton's technical artistry and craftsmanship whilst embracing nostalgic design cues. Simply put, it's a modern incarnation of the past.

Being a prototype, some details of the V4CR may well change, so for now we can only wait for the full specification to be released when finalised.

In the meantime, here are a few key features for you:

CARBON FIBRE FUEL TANK AND BODY PANELS | POLISHED BILLET ALUMINIUM SWINGARM AND FRAME | ENGINE DEVELOPED IN-HOUSE; SHARING THE SAME ENGINE AS THE NORTON V4SV | SHORTER ALUMINIUM REAR FRAME | COMPACT TAIL UNIT AND POSITIONING OF EXHAUST ALL CONTRIBUTE TOWARDS THE V4CR'S AGGRESSIVE AND DOMINANT STANCE | TRADITIONALLY LARGE, ROUND HEADLAMP FITTED WITH A MODERN LED UNIT | VISIBLE FRAMEWORK AND DISTINGUISHED WELDS SHOWCASE ATTENTION TO DETAIL

THE BACKGROUND

Norton Motorcycles was founded in 1898 as a manufacturer of fittings and parts to the two-wheel trade. It went on to become one of the most iconic British motorcycle brands, manufacturing famous models such as the 650SS, Atlas, Commando, Dominator, Manx, Navigator and more – constantly innovating in motorcycle technology, with features advantageous for lightness and strength in motorcycle racing. With an unrivalled history in motorsport, the brand name is synonymous with Isle of Man TT racing.

In April 2020, Norton Motorcycles was acquired by TVS Motor Company, India's third largest motorcycle manufacturer. Under the leadership of TVS, Norton is based out of a new manufacturing facility in Solihull, West Midlands, building British bikes in England using traditional handcrafted techniques with modern-day machinery for consistently high quality.

WHITE COLLAR KAWASAKI

ndonesia may not outwardly appear to be a hotbed of café racer culture, but the radical and unique build from Ram Ram Januar at White Collar Bike in Bandung, West Java, defies that notion. Using a Kawasaki Vulcan 650 engine as a stressed member, Ram made his own frame from 8mm steel plate, with a separate tubular subframe to support the seat and tail, while the bodywork is also handmade from sheet aluminium. Suspension and braking are courtesy of Ducati parts, with a Panigale front end and a swinging arm and wheel from an 848, with wheels being the delightful Kineo spoked items. To allow the Vulcan engine to perform at its best, the standard fuel injection was dispensed with and replaced with a pair of gaping Lectron carburettors, allied to the free-flowing stainless steel exhausts.
– Dave Manning **CRI**

2022 KTM 790 DUKE

THE ORIGINAL SCALPEL RETURNS

motorcycle with ready-to-race character and performance.

Neatly filling the gap between the 390 Duke and 890 Duke, Europe receives the 95hp version, allowing for A2 configuration. The rest of the world will receive the full 105hp version. Motorcycles will arrive on dealer floors from June.

The latter is powered by the most compact twin-cylinder in its class, generating 105hp and 87Nm. This has been tuned specifically for torque output, providing easy, rideable power. However, an impressive top-end ensures the 790 Duke maintains its excitement throughout the rev-range while meagre fuel consumption of only 64mpg (4.4 l/100km)

The KTM 790 Duke has made a welcome return to the streets, bringing a renewed rebellious streak to the world of midweight naked machinery.

From its inception in 2017, the 790 Duke took worldwide motorcycle markets by storm, selling over 29,000 units. This was followed by the introduction of the KTM 890 Duke R, labelled the Super Scalpel, placing the KTM LC8c parallel-twin engine at the top of the food chain of the middleweights. In early 2021, the 90 Duke was upgraded to the KTM 890 Duke, with more power and improved electronics.

The 2022 790 Duke is the continuation of that story which introduced the world to the power and agility of the KTM LC8c parallel-twin platform, with further development offering a true global midrange

means riders can enjoy the twisties long before the fuel light flashes.

A lot of attention was also paid to ensure the typical Duke riding feeling of lightness, agility and sportiness. Handling is not only agile, but also precise, thanks to geometry developed specifically for sporty street riding. High-quality WP Apex suspension at each end ensures a perfect connection with the road, and rider confidence at all times.

Like a middleweight boxer in his or her prime, the 2022 790 Duke will no doubt prove to be a champion of merging agility and hard-hitting punch. More so, it continues the trend of being a leader in the market when it comes to power-to-weight ratio and equipment levels.

The usual selection of ride modes, notably Rain, Street and Sport settings, provide riders with easy-to-access customisation of traction and throttle control, ensuring confident riding in all road and weather conditions.

In terms of looks, the bike introduces two new colours to the mix, with a traditional KTM orange scheme and an all-new grey and black motif entering the fray. **CRI**

'GRIND MACHINE' ART-BIKE VISION SET TO BECOME A REALITY

Indian Motorcycle, in collaboration with Wheels and Waves, commissioned four European builders to design its vision of an Indian Chief inspired from the past, anchored in the present, and looking towards the future.

The winning design, chosen through a combination of public vote and a panel of 'super voters' (see who they were on the following page) can be revealed as GRIND Machine by Tank Machine.

As the winning design in the competition, Tank Machine will now build GRIND Machine in time to be presented to one lucky winner during their VIP trip to the 2022 Wheels and Waves festival north of Biarritz, France.

The annual five-day, multi-site event, which takes place from June 29 to July 3, continues to be inspired by motorcycle culture and shaken by its various influences.

Relying on the past, on 'savoir faire' to live the present and talk about the future, you can enjoy a mix of influences, with bikes, surfing, music and art on the menu. Check out further details at www.wheels-and-waves.com/en/biarritz-2022/

THE DESIGNERS

The concept Tank Machine is a workshop in the Paris region founded in 2015 by Clément Molina specialising in motorcycle design, customisation and the development of Plug & Play Kits.

The workshop has always had a special link with the Indian Motorcycle brand and Wheels and Waves, which is why the Tank Machine team has joined forces with Antonin Bazin from the 'RiseDesign.fr' agency to merge their 'board culture.

Snapshot

THE SUPER VOTER PANEL

Surrounded by choppers and hot rods from a young age on the family farm in Sweden, **Ola Stenegärd** has been part of the long-established Swedish chopper and custom scene all of his life, with many world-famous builds to his name.

Ola's innate feel of lines and stance has been honed from a long study and appreciation of all the builders and designers around the world. With a Masters in Applied Art (industrial design) his working design life started with cars. But Ola was destined to return to motorcycles and joined Indian Motorcycle in 2001 during the Gilroy years. After moving on to progress through the industry, Ola returned to Indian Motorcycle in 2018 as director of industrial design and was honoured to be assigned to lead the team that would reimagine the iconic Indian Chief for its 100th anniversary.

From Long Beach, California, **Roland Sands'** first dirt bike was given to him on his fifth birthday. His love of speed on two wheels took him to the professional racing ranks for 10 years, setting multiple track records and becoming 1998 American Motorcyclist Association 250GP champion. Roland traded in his racing leathers for hammer, pencil, and computer design to build motorcycles and custom motorcycle products, founding Roland Sands Design in 2005. Playing a pivotal role in popularising high-performance custom bikes to the masses, his designs have earned many awards through the years as well as featuring in over 500 magazine articles worldwide and on over a hundred covers.

Paul d'Orléans is a globally recognised expert on motorcycle history and culture. He founded *The Vintagent* as a blog in October 2006, sensing a new opportunity to explore imagery and ideas. The immediate popularity of The Vintagent led him to abandon a 25-year career as a decorative paint specialist by 2009, in favour of a new career of writing, photography and film, mostly related to motorcycles.

Michael Lichter is a commercial photographer based in

Boulder, Colorado, who specialises in motorcycle photography. He has been capturing the bikes, the people and the attitude since 1977 when he realised he was a better photographer than drummer and left the BeBop band he was in. By 1979, Easyriders was publishing his work and in the years since, assignments have taken him around the globe many times over.

Tadashi Kono has been creating articles about motorcycles as a freelancer for over 20 years for both magazines and digital media. More than 25 years ago, he joined the editorial office of a motorcycle magazine that focused on vintage and custom motorcycles. Alongside an editorial office stocked with old books and photographs about many motorcycles, colleagues who were full of experience and knowledge, and the need to have multiple abilities, Tadashi was able to acquire all the skills he needed to work as a freelancer. In 2015, Tadashi started to cover custom motorcycle shows such as Wheels and Waves in France and Glemseck in Germany, as well as Bike Shed London, Pure and Crafted, Auerberg Klassik, Throttle Roll, and One Moto Show.

Katharina Weber entered the motorcycle world in 1996 as a trainee at a German publisher. It was the heyday of customising. Motorcycles had fat tyres and black paintwork, and the first years she worked in the editorial office of *Bikers News*, a one percenter rocker magazine. In 2005 she switched to *Custombike*, one of Europe's oldest print magazines for customised motorcycles.

In 2013 Katharina became editor-in-chief for the magazine. Over 15 years she built up a network of professional and private bike builders, photographers, writers and chroniclers of the custom motorcycle scene. After the bankruptcy of the old publisher in 2020, Katharina and a small team of enthusiasts published *Custombike* and the partner magazine *Dream-machines* independently.

RADICAL INDIAN FTR BLACK SWAN BY WORKSHOP SPEED SHOP

Indian Motorcycle and Workhorse Speed Shop have revealed the second of two special Indian FTR builds. Hot on the heels of the Workhorse FTR AMA comes Black Swan, a different – but no less radical – take on what can be achieved with the FTR.

Black Swan was a concept that Workhorse founder, Brice Hennebert, conceived several years ago when racing at Wheels and Waves against Miracle Mike, the Indian Scout by The Young Guns.

As with the Workhorse FTR AMA build, the style inspirations come from multiple directions and eras, 1990s superbikes, modern Grand Prix racers, and even Rauh-Welt tuned Porsches.

"During that time, I had the vision to build a sports bike for road use, really sporty, built like a GP bike. It's deeply inspired by 90s sports bikes, all made from carbon fibre. The owner of the bike gave me total freedom around the project. So, I pushed all the levels to my maximum. That's what happens when I have total freedom from the commissioners of a project. It's pretty unique and the most complicated build I've done to date," said Brice.

After preliminary sketches, he took a trip to Akrapovic HQ in Solvenia to help fabricate the beautiful 2-1 exhaust system, with the underslung muffler keeping the sleek profile Brice envisioned.

Back at his workshop, having narrowly avoided being delayed in Solvenia by the closed borders happening around the world at the time, Brice constructed a wire mesh around the FTR as a base on which to model the bodywork in clay.

"This step was actually easier than I expected because I did not need to create a full symmetric body in clay, just one half of the bike as a master. Once I was happy with the shape, I used a 3D scanner to pass the form to Formae Design who worked with me to refine the virtual model, create the full-body symmetry, and integrate all the accessories and fittings. Christophe at Formae helped me a lot with all the

different components of the body."

While Formae perfected the body design, Brice turned to chassis modifications such as the fuel tank fabrication around the original air intake system. Tim from Vinco Racing Engineering helped with a lot of CNC machined components from Brice's designs such as the swingarm fitting, chassis plates, triple trees, fuel cell components and more.

When the CAD model of the one-piece body was finalised, it was 3D printed and passed to Robert Colyns from 13.8 Composites, a master in carbon fibre fabrication. 13.8 Composites worked on

Snapshot

the print to create a perfect surface from which to produce a mould for the one-piece body.

"As I'd decided to show off the carbon fibre and not paint it, I gave Robert the freedom to choose the carbon weave that would look the best and still work with the design I had given him. After a few weeks of waiting, he came back with this hell of a piece. The whole body only weighs about 1.8kg. Creating the bodywork was a major part of the build, everything but practical, but I was determined to have a one-piece body."

With the body now realised, including an aluminium bellypan for better resistance to exhaust heat, Brice now had to implement one of his primary ideas, a system to

dramatically reveal and hide the headlight.

"That was one hell of a struggle for me. It may look simple and easy for some people, but for me, that was quite a challenge. The 'eyelids' are driven by two stepper motors controlled by a Arduino for cinematic opening and closing."

With the carbon body, closed 'eyelids' and the 3D printed elements on the body, Black Swan really lives up to its name. The use of 3D printing – a feature that Black Swan shares with the FTR AMA build – allowed Brice to accent the body shape quickly and simply in a 'wink' to the wide-body kits in Japan, mixing high-performance competition style and street mods.

Always looking to add as much fabrication to a build as possible, the details that set Workhorse builds apart, Brice fabricated a new swingarm from 7020 aluminium. Retaining the original suspension mounting point, Öhlins Racing provided a special piggyback shock in black to match the overall theme, complemented by special black front forks.

"The braking system is from my partner

Beringer. They offered the use of a prototype system, one of the lightest braking systems they have. It's about 1kg for the complete front wheel system, all connected to the Rotobox carbon wheels with Dunlop-supplied GP Racer tyres for a perfect connection to the ground. This bike is really dynamic on the streets."

CHARGE OF THE RIGHT BRIGADE

Battery failure is an all-too-common reason for a roadside rescue. *CRI* talked to battery-saving experts at Optimate to find out why optimisers make sense for bikes, including, of course, café racers.

Year-in, year-out, batteries are the number one reason for a call to the recovery man. The AA and RAC respond to around 500,000 battery-related breakdowns and replace about 150,000 at the roadside every year. Yes, those numbers include cars as well as bikes, but you get the point.

A popular misconception is that as we're not using our bikes as much – for most of us, motorcycles have become a leisure pursuit rather than everyday transport – and our batteries aren't taking as much of a hammering, but nothing could be further from the truth.

Even if you put a new lead-acid battery on the shelf in your garage and leave it, the chemical reaction inside will happen – albeit in a tiny amount – and eventually it will go flat. If that battery is connected to a bike – with a digital clock flashing away,

an alarm or on-board computer running – then that process will speed up and the battery will flatten in no time.

The same goes for lithium-ion batteries. They need to be kept within a strict voltage range all the time. Overcharge one and it can heat up and eventually self-destruct: Burning from the inside out; leave it without charge and it will flatten much quicker than a lead-acid battery and can be difficult to recover.

So, how do we stop that from happening? Regularly charging and maintaining your battery massively helps prolong its working life and will reduce the likelihood of breakdowns significantly. Before you dig out your dad's 1950 voltmaster 3000 from the back of the garage, remember that things have moved on a little.

Step one is to find out what type of battery is fitted to your bike. Conventional lead acid batteries will usually be labelled with reference numbers starting with the letters YB, CB or GB (eg, YB14L-A2); Y, C or G (eg, Y60-N24L-A); or 12N (eg, 12N24-3).

Maintenance-free or AGM (absorbed glass mat) batteries are the most common type used in modern bikes, and normally have reference numbers starting with the letters YTX, CTX or GTX (eg, YTX9-BS).

Lithium-ion batteries will generally be marked as 'Li-ion', 'LFP' or 'LiFePO4'.

Why is this important? Because using the wrong type of charger can at best leave your battery still flat in the morning and at worst can damage it beyond repair.

Step two used to be checking the condition of your battery using a multimeter, but these days battery optimisers – like those

Finishing touches were provided by Jeroen from Silver Machine Seats.

"I would never have achieved such a complicated build alone. So many of my previous partners on Appaloosa stepped up to the plate, as well as a host of others, and I thank them all. I got a lot of pleasure working on this project and I hope that Black Swan gives the owner, and anyone who sees it, the same feeling." **CRI**

from the OptiMate range – test charge, maintain and can even repair a bike's battery, completely automatically. All you need to do is pick the right one.

The OptiMate 5 Select will save, charge and maintain all 6V and 12V lead-acid batteries. Designed to eliminate the need for multiple chargers – and the risk of attaching them to the wrong machine – simply connect the OptiMate5 to the vehicle battery, select the appropriate voltage and it does the rest automatically.

If you're running a newer bike – or more than one – the OptiMate 1 Duo is the one for you. It works with both new AGM (sealed lead-acid) or lithium batteries, using the very latest in charging technology to automatically determine the type of battery it's connected to, and selecting the charging programme to suit, so you don't have to.

If you're lucky enough to have several bikes, OptiMate's O-125 Monitor makes it easy to keep an eye on the condition of all their batteries. Just attach one to the battery and you can instantly see the charge level on an easy-to-read LED display panel. It will also tell you if your charging system is working correctly.

Visit **www.optimate1. com** to see the company's full range. **CRI**

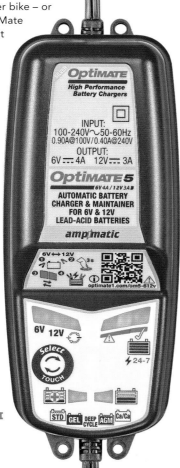

HONDA UPDATES CB300R:
The Japanese factory has revealed the latest update to its extensive Neo Sports Café range, with a tweaked version of its learner-legal CB300R. The big news for the A2-compliant bike is the addition of 41mm Showa forks up front, an assist/slipper clutch, and some tweaks to its 286cc liquid-cooled engine to help it meet Euro 5 emissions regulations. Alongside the CB1000R, CB650R and CB125R, Honda's CB300R is a stripped-back machine with sharp, futuristic styling that's proved popular among style-conscious riders who don't want to compromise performance. Pop across to pages 44-47 for more information.

INDIAN SCOUT GOES ROGUE:
Indian Motorcycle has unleashed the most aggressive and attitude-packed iteration of its iconic Indian Scout – the new Scout Rogue. New features include a quarter fairing, mini ape-hanger handlebars, sport-style seat, blacked-out fenders and valve covers, and a 19-inch front wheel. Delivering 70kW (94hp) by way of a liquid-cooled, 1133cc (69 cubic inch) V-twin motor, the model comes in sagebrush smoke, black smoke midnight and stealth grey, and is available in A2 compliant specification for new riders. Interested? We are! You can find more on pages 112-119.

ROUGH CRAFTS ENFIELD

Royal Enfield's air-cooled parallel twin engine that has recently proved so incredibly popular, is set to become one of the most suitable engines for customisers in the near future. Not only is it pretty to look at, but the fuel-injected powerplant doesn't have anywhere near as much electronics as other manufacturers' offerings and is consequently much easier to customise. Winston Yeh of Rough Crafts in Taiwan was commissioned by Royal Enfield to build a performance machine from a standard Continental GT model, and the end result is a modern machine with modern suspension and brakes, but with an iconic profile that belies the fact that some modern, lightweight materials have been used in its construction. – *Dave Manning* **CRI**

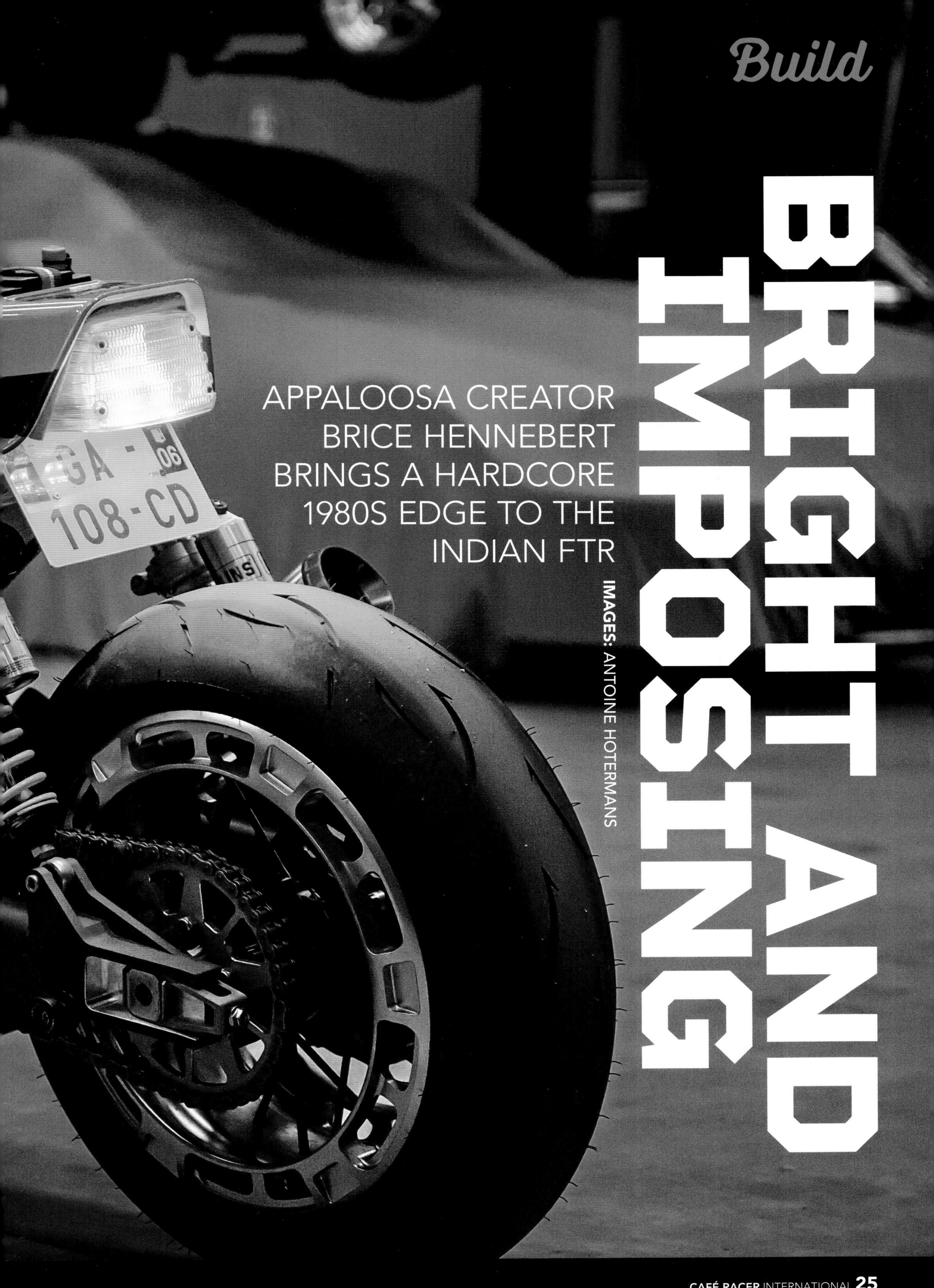

BRIGHT AND IMPOSING

APPALOOSA CREATOR
BRICE HENNEBERT
BRINGS A HARDCORE
1980S EDGE TO THE
INDIAN FTR

IMAGES: ANTOINE HOTERMANS

THE BRIEF WAS PRETTY OPEN, SOMETHING COLOURFUL AND AS SHARP AS A WAR TANK

Indian Motorcycle and Workhorse Speed Shop have revealed the FTR AMA, the first of two long-anticipated Indian FTR builds by Brice Hennebert, creator of Appaloosa, the Indian Scout-based sprint racer.

Well known for his unique creations, and with two iterations of Appaloosa already under his belt, Brice was commissioned to create two very special FTRs – Black Swan and the FTR AMA – for two brothers.

While Black Swan is yet to be revealed, it was the commissioner of Black Swan who asked Brice to design a second build for his brother. The result is the FTR AMA, a bright and imposing motorcycle with a hardcore, 1980s edge.

"The brief was pretty open, something colourful and as sharp as a war tank," said Brice. "The only restriction was that the paint be inspired by the Martini Racing livery. After some research and brainstorming with myself, I based the look around AMA SBK racers from the 1980s and the rally cars from the same era. The main influences were the Lancia Delta HF mixed with Bol d'Or 750s and some muscle bike DNA."

Starting work in early February 2021, Brice's first decision was to retain an upright riding position, something close to the original FTR and using the original handlebars. From there, a lot of changes were about to happen.

"While Black Swan was a clay-shaped build, I decided to go in another direction in terms of design process with this bike. I used direct CAD design based on a 3D scan of the FTR chassis. Then, all the body parts were 3D printed and reinforced with carbon fibre."

The 3D printed front plate houses a PiAA race light and supports the Setrab oil cooler beneath. Nestled behind the front plate sits the OEM dash from the new Indian Chief, a design more in keeping with the retro racing mood, but with all the options of a modern machine, such as phone connection and charging.

The printed module that incorporates the seat pan and tail light is also the battery holder, the battery having been moved into the rear as a nod to endurances bikes. With the

saddle upholstered in a smooth brushed leather by long-time collaborator, Jeroen from Silver Machine, the tail section is complemented by an old school tail light adapted to take LEDs.

To accommodate the DNA performance air filters, the intake was redesigned and 3D printed, while two aluminium fuel cells were fabricated to fit the new bodywork; one under the tank cover and the other hung under the seat unit. Connected by AN10 connectors, the capacity matches the fourteen litres of the original bike.

The chassis plates were redesigned for a more race-like look and machined from Brice's CAD designs by Vinco Racing in Holland. Vinco Racing undertook all the machining on the project including the swingarm components, braking brackets, yokes, fuel cell components, the front brackets for oil cooler, and more.

Vinco Racing spent a great deal of time on the machining, which saved Brice the time to focus on other areas.

The fork yokes are replicas of Bol d'Or 750cc yokes adapted to the 43mm Öhlins forks. And at the rear the tail section was modified to use twin piggyback Öhlins shocks mated to a bespoke swingarm built from 7020 aluminium tubes. The swingarm design was inspired by the same era and is 40mm longer compared with the original, with a 3D printed chain slider protecting the tubing.

"The wheel set is a total eye-catcher. I collaborated with Fabio from JoNich Wheels in Italy; the design is based on his Rush wheels, machined from billet aluminium, but without the carbon flanges. The design makes me think about the turbo fans wheels used on the racing Lancia. So that was a perfect choice for me. They are completed by a Dunlop GP tyre set with this mad 200 rear tyre."

Clearance for the braking system was a concern with these wheels, so Brice called on another long-time collaborator, Etienne at Beringer Brakes.

"I called Etienne to get their 4D braking system, the same system I used on Appaloosa. Etienne is always motivated for technical challenges. So, we played with different colours on the components to work with the AMA mood. And then, because I removed the ABS module, I had to find another way to get the speed signal on the bike and the solution was a Motogadget Moto Scope Mini."

To create the swoop of the exhaust, it was fabricated from stainless steel pie cuts and beautifully welded together, capped off by a couple of modified slip-on S&S Cycle Grand National mufflers.

"The amazing paint job designed by Axecent in Japan has been applied by my friend Fabian who's near to my workshop. This build is aggressive, massive and a real pleasure to ride. I had a lot of fun testing it." **CRI**

A&J
TRIUMPH
THRUXTON

Being a company that specialises in twin cylinder Triumphs from the Hinckley factory, A&J Cycles in New York likes to have its own bike with which to undertake development work, and to showcase its products to the paying public. This 2007 Triumph Thruxton has had a number of guises over the years, with this café racer version being the latest iteration.

Brian Ballard and his team at A&J have upgraded the 900cc twin and incorporated GSX-R forks and radial brakes, an aluminium Calfab swinging arm, Nitron shocks, 17-inch Excel wheel rims and some sticky Dunlop rubber to turn the original bike into a lightweight corner-carving café racer, while the addition of a two-into-one stainless exhaust and a pair of Keihin FCR flatslides give the engine the power to match.
– *Dave Manning* **CRI**

THE BIG PAYOFF

SUBTLE STYLING WITH A FOCUS ON HANDLING AND PERFORMANCE

HART-BERNTHAL COLLABORATION

"THESE 116 MOTORS ARE NO JOKE, THESE THINGS RUN LIKE A CHAMPION AND THE BIKE REALLY LENDS ITSELF TO CUSTOMISING AND MAKING IT YOUR OWN" – CAREY HART

Indian Motorcycle has revealed the custom Indian Chief built by Carey Hart for actor Jon Bernthal, the third and final build commissioned to showcase the vast customisation possibilities of the all-new Indian Chief.

As a former freestyle motocross competitor and motorcycle racer, Carey's builds are inspired from his MX world. "I love performance, I love going fast, turning fast and braking hard," said Carey. "I don't sacrifice anything on my bikes that is going to jeopardise their handling, how it performs, or my safety.

"I was really excited to hear about the new Chief when it was announced, that they were sticking to the old aesthetic – you know, dual shocks, triangular steel frame, the stance of the bike, how the bike handles, the power. These 116 motors are no joke, these things run like a champion and the bike really lends itself to customising and making it your own."

To steer the direction and build the perfect bike, Carey got to know Jon prior to, and during, the build so that he could understand his influences and what he's interested in. The ergonomic set up was also helped by the fact that Jon and Carey are of very similar height and size, allowing Carey to size up the riding position himself. "I just wanted him to fit in the bike like a glove," said Carey.

Jon commented: "I was immediately blown away by how good a guy he is. I knew I was doing this with one of the best in the world. So, it's just like trusting his expression, getting to know me, what kind of guy I am and the things that are important to me. And that's what really interested me about this opportunity.

"There's so much that excites me about it. The basic set up of it is perfect. Where the handlebars sit, how he's lifted it a little bit. I wanted it to be kind of exactly what it is. I wanted it to be humble, but elegant. I didn't want the bike to draw too much attention to itself, but when you looked at it a little bit closer you realised how special it is. I think it's beautiful. I can't imagine a more perfect bike. I can't believe that I get to ride this thing."

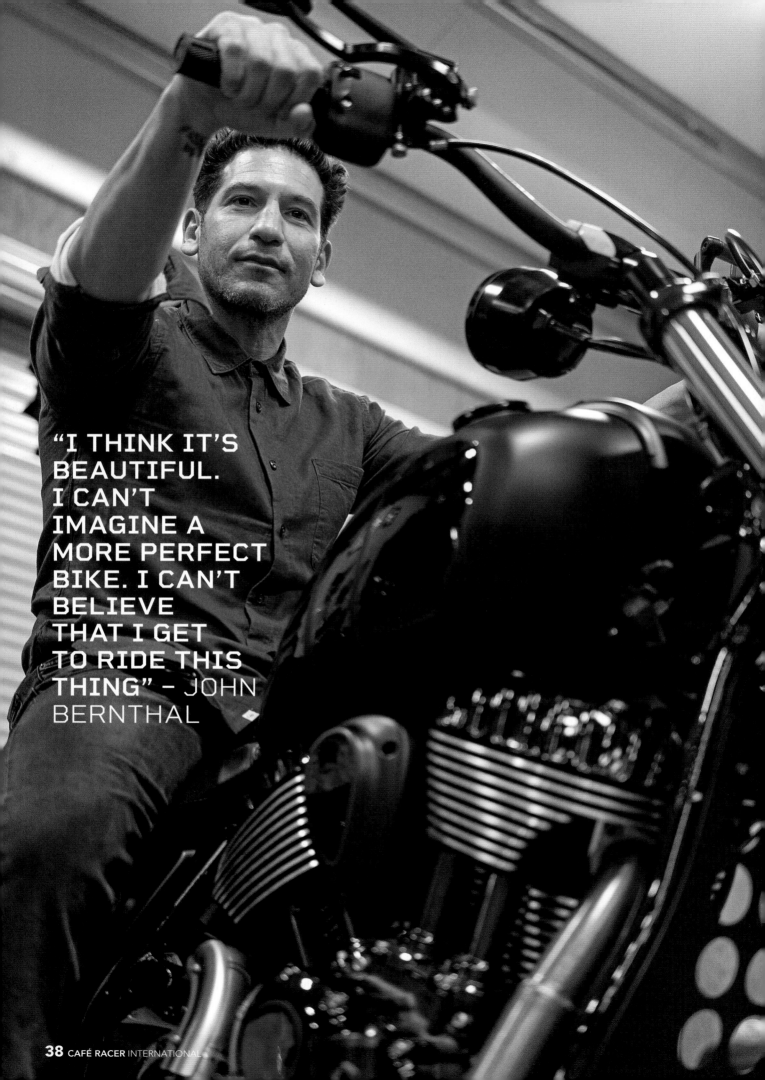

"I THINK IT'S BEAUTIFUL. I CAN'T IMAGINE A MORE PERFECT BIKE. I CAN'T BELIEVE THAT I GET TO RIDE THIS THING" – JOHN BERNTHAL

This was the first time Cary had built a motorcycle for someone else, so it was definitely a little bit of a nail-biter for him. "Seeing his excitement over the motorcycle, seeing his appreciation for the time that me and Big B put in on the motorcycle and just knowing that he's genuinely, genuinely happy about the bike and that the bike is going to see a lot of road miles, that was just the big payoff for me.

"I'm really happy with the motorcycle. I wanted the bike to handle well; I wanted him to be comfortable in the saddle. I wanted him to just be able to be one with that motorcycle. I think with the end result, both visually and how the bike stands and sits, I feel like I really accomplished that." **CRI**

Specification

KRAUS BAR CLAMPS, RISERS AND GAUGE BRACKET | ODI BARS & ODI/HARTLUCK LOCK ON GRIPS | PRO BOLT TITANIUM HARDWARE | DRAG SPECIALTIES LICENCE PLATE BRACKET | CUSTOM LOWER FRAME COVER | BERINGER FRONT BRAKE MASTER AND CLUTCH PERCH | BARNETT CLUTCH CABLE | GALFER FRONT BRAKE LINE | BERINGER FRONT AND REAR BRAKE CALLIPERS | GALFER FRONT AND REAR BRAKE ROTORS | SAN DIEGO CUSTOMS WHEELS | DUNLOP TYRES | SAN DIEGO CUSTOMS SHIFT/BRAKE PEGS | SADDLEMEN HART LUCK SEAT | RIZOMA MIRRORS | RIZOMA REAR BRAKE LIGHTS AND FRONT INDICATOR LIGHTS | AIRTRIX PAINT | FOX PIGGYBACK SHOCKS +1 INCH | CUSTOM MACHINED INSPECTION COVER | FAB 28 2-INTO-1 STAINLESS EXHAUST | ROKFORM PHONE MOUNT | GP SUSPENSION FOR REVALVE

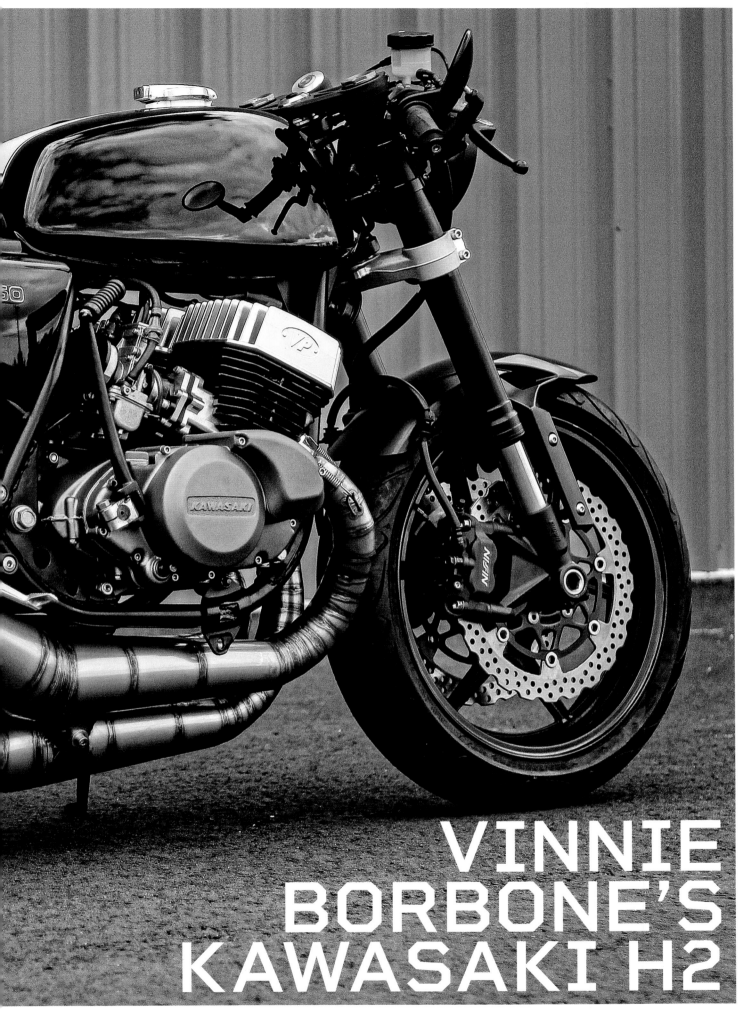

VINNIE BORBONE'S KAWASAKI H2

While Vinnie Borbone isn't the first person to use a race-prepped engine in his café racer, there are probably very few who have taken that ex-race powerplant and then rebuilt it to have even more radical tuning for its subsequent road use! Having raced his Kawasaki H2, with the constraints that are brought about by classic racing regulations, Vinnie could fit modern rolling gear (from a variety of Kawasaki production race replicas) as well as modern go-faster goodies such as the Wiseco pistons, billet cylinder heads, Mikuni flat-slide carbs, Fast From The Past stainless steel exhausts, and a new crank from Vintco.com   The result is a classic Kawasaki café racer with a bit of crackle that'll set the twisting highways of New Hampshire alight! – *Dave Manning* **CRI**

PURE
ROADSTER
ATTITUDE

HONDA CB300R

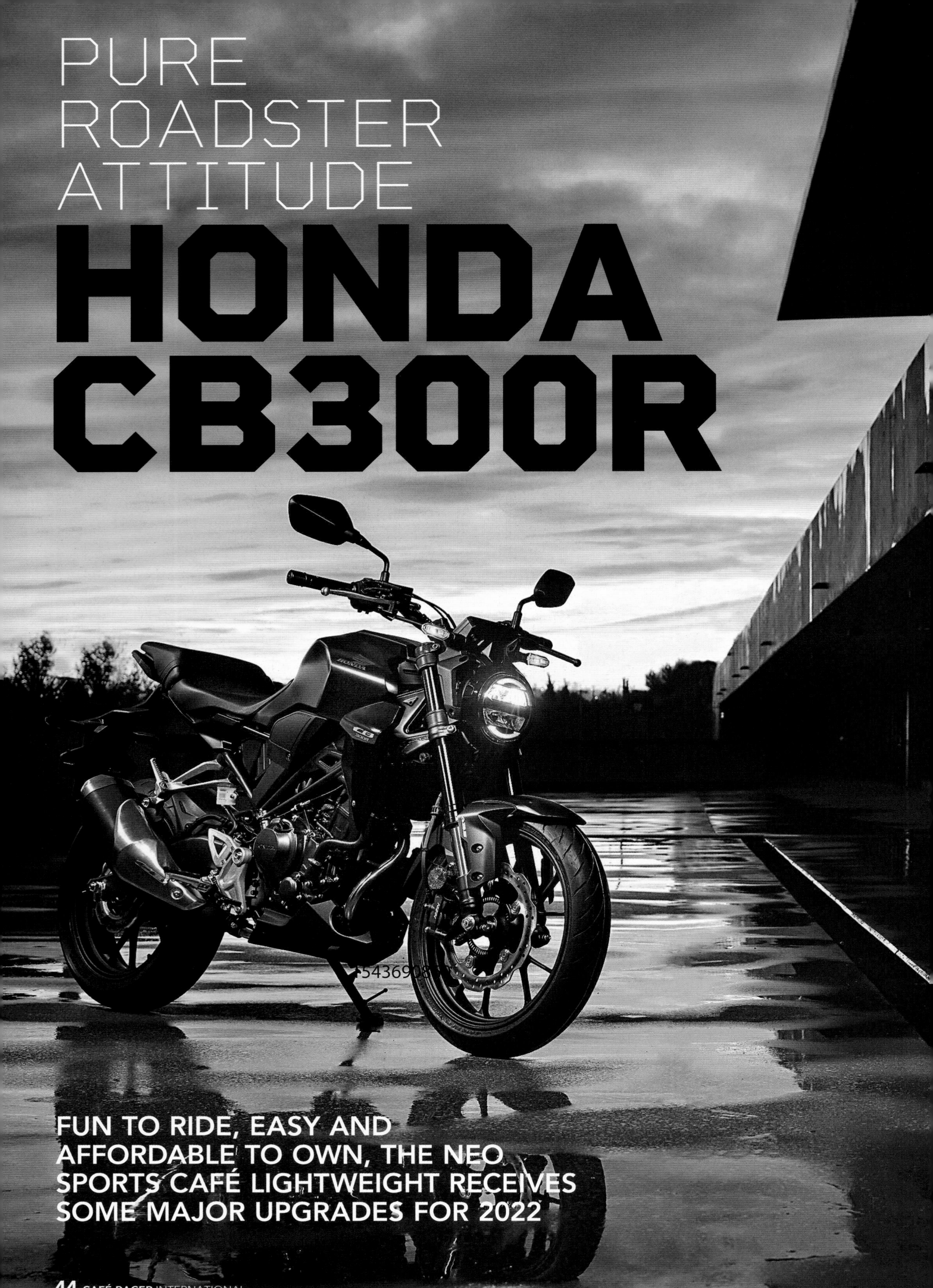

FUN TO RIDE, EASY AND
AFFORDABLE TO OWN, THE NEO
SPORTS CAFÉ LIGHTWEIGHT RECEIVES
SOME MAJOR UPGRADES FOR 2022

Strip motorcycling down to its bare essentials and often less equals more. Honda has long understood this, and in 2018 created the CB300R. Part of the Neo Sports Café family – which includes the flagship CB1000R, A1 licence-friendly CB125R and recently updated CB650R four-cylinder middleweight – it distils all of the excitement of two wheels into lightweight form.

Very much a first 'big' bike for young or new riders after a 125cc machine, it offers engaging response and sensations from both engine and chassis without the weight, cost and licence implications of a larger-capacity motorcycle. Conversely, the CB300R also offers an attractive proposition for experienced riders looking to downsize.

Fun to ride, easy and affordable to own, the CB300R has received some major upgrades for 2022, including high-quality front suspension; assist/slipper clutch; and Euro5 compliance for the engine. Just as before, it brings unique style to Europe's city streets, with a bare-boned attitude that is guaranteed to turn heads.

The CB300R tips the scales at a wet weight of just 144kg, giving Honda's small-bore bike an immediate performance advantage. Mix in a free-revving 286cc liquid-cooled single cylinder engine and the unique Neo Sports Café naked bike presence, and the CB300R has the perfect formula to both excite and inspire riders.

VALERIO AIELLO OF HONDA'S ROME R&D DEPARTMENT ON THE NEO SPORTS CAFÉ DESIGN AESTHETIC:

"The entire current Neo Sports Café range from Honda is the result of the CB4 Concept model presented at EICMA in 2015. Our desire was to explore the world of the café racer and reinterpret it in a modern key.

"All the models of this CB series are not simply retro-vintage motorcycles, but rather neo-classics – that is, modern motorbikes showcasing classic design styles combined with modern techniques.

"We wanted to create a new stylistic dimension, different from the muscular streetfighters of the last few years, and at the same time, far from the simpler café racer style. The end result is that none of the bikes from the competition resemble the Neo Sports Café range and, like them or not, they are easily recognisable as Hondas. The competitors have classic or very modern motorcycles in their ranges, but in my opinion, not something that goes in the wake of both styles.

"During development of the CB4 concept, I found inspiration from outside the world of motorcycles, in watches. I've always liked their technicality and one of the key concepts used during the Neo Sports Café design was 'mechanical art' – the desire to show the beauty of the various mechanical elements to which Honda has always given great importance. Watches do this very well indeed, with their mechanics always creating a certain charm."

Specification

HONDA CB300R | £4899

ENGINE: 286CC LIQUID-COOLED FOUR-VALVE DOHC SINGLE | **POWER:** 22.9KW @ 9,000RPM | **TORQUE:** 27.5NM @ 7750RPM | **TRANSMISSION:** SIX-SPEED | **FRAME:** STEEL DIAMOND | **FRONT SUSPENSION:** 41MM SHOWA SEPARATE FUNCTION FRONTFORK BIG PISTON (SFF-BP) USD FORKS. 130MM STROKE | **REAR SUSPENSION:** MONOSHOCK DAMPER WITH FIVE-STAGE ADJUSTABLE PRELOAD, 107MM TRAVEL | **FRONT BRAKE:** 296MM HUBLESS FLOATING DISC WITH RADIAL-MOUNT NISSIN FOUR-PISTON CALLIPER | **REAR BRAKE:** 220MM DISC WITH SINGLE PISTON CALLIPER | **FRONT TYRE:** 110/70R17M/C 54H | **REAR TYRE:** 150/60R17M/C 65H | **SEAT HEIGHT:** 700MM | **FUEL CAPACITY:** 10 LITRES | **FUEL CONSUMPTION:** 30.2KM/LITRE | **KERB WEIGHT:** 144KG | **CONTACT:** WWW.HONDA.CO.UK

Underpinning the CB300R's minimalism is its tubular and pressed steel construction diamond-style frame. The swingarm is manufactured from steel plate, irregularly shaped in cross-section. Both are designed to achieve high longitudinal rigidity and control torsion from wheel deflection without excess rigidity or weight. The chassis' core strength is anchored by the pressed steel swingarm pivot plates and swingarm, allowing the frame to deliver agile handling with stability and feedback.

The CB300R now features, as standard equipment, 41mm Showa Separate Function front Fork Big Piston (SFF-BP) USD forks (the same high-quality specification as fitted to the CB650R, with spring rate and damping changes), as well as a radial-mounted Nissin four-piston calliper; 296mm hubless floating front disc; the rear 220mm disc via a single-piston calliper; IMU-controlled ABS; and radial tyres. The high-specification system works through an IMU (inertial measurement unit) to give precise front and rear distribution of ABS

operation depending on the bike's behaviour. A 150/60R-17 radial rear tyre matches the 110/70R-17 radial front.

A 49.6% front/50.4% rear weight bias provides a positive feel for front-end grip and easy steering, which is also helped by the low, 144kg wet weight and compact 1352mm wheelbase. Seat height is set at 799mm.

The CB300R's styling is true to Honda's Neo Sports Café naked bike design language, putting the bike's blacked-out hardware on display. It's brutally neat; the cutaway tail unit is barely there and supports separate rider and pillion seat. The seat features a new revised cover thickness for additional comfort and both rider and pillion foot peg hangers are aluminium.

A thin (23.5mm and weighing just 230g) full function LCD instrument display provides speed, engine rpm and fuel level, with gear position now highlighted in its own, negative form. Warning lights are arranged across the top. Full LED lighting – including indicators – gives a premium feel and contributes to mass centralisation. The headlight uses a dual bar light signature, upper for low beam and lower for high beam, and the tail light is extremely thin.

The 10-litre fuel tank is hidden underneath an angular cover and shrouds and houses an aircraft-style filler cap. With fuel economy of 30.2km/l (WMTC mode), the CB300R can cover over 320km from full.

The CB300R's compact, 286cc DOHC four-valve liquid-cooled single cylinder engine is a diminutive jewel that has won many fans for its free-revving and responsive nature. And while it may pump adrenaline as revs rise, it's also an engine that works well in real-world road riding conditions, around town or out on the highway. Peak power of 22.9kW arrives @ 9000rpm, with peak torque of 27.5Nm delivered @ 7750rpm.

New for this year, an assist/slipper clutch allows super-smooth shifts and manages rear wheel 'hop' on rapid downshifting and hard braking. The six-speed gearbox offers an even spread of gears for strong acceleration and the gear change mechanism employs an adjustable rose joint linkage.

For Euro5 compliance – alongside an OBD2-compatible crank sensor – the underslung exhaust mid-section has been redesigned and incorporates a new larger catalyser. The right-side exit muffler also features a new, simpler internal structure. **CRI**

HIGH-CLASS STREET PERFORMER

INDIAN FTR R CARBON

WORDS: MICHAEL COWTON
IMAGES: INDIAN MOTORCYCLE
AND GETAPIC.CO.UK

IF YOU ARE SEEKING A PLANTED,
ENGAGING RIDE WITH OODLES OF STREET
APPEAL, THEN YOU COULD DO A LOT WORSE
THAN THIS STUNNING HEAD-TURNER

Ridden

THE STRIKING NAKED BEAUTY BRINGS TO THE TABLE THE FLAGSHIP MODEL IN THE FTR LINE-UP

When I was a child my friends and I would play Cowboys and Indians: Innocent war games of a different type to those enjoyed by the kids of today as they go google-eyed at computer screens. I had a home-made bow and arrow (blunted end, but it didn't travel far anyway). My friends wore frilled trousers and sported US Marshal badges made of cheap tin. I would wear a bandana with a pigeon feather stuck in the back, and imagined I was Chief Sitting Bull. Or maybe I was a scout as I tore around on my bicycle. I can't really remember. No matter, those days are long gone, although the images of innocence linger.

It took me a long time to realise that Indians, chiefs and scouts remain on the agenda, if only of the two-wheeled variety. And boy, have I been missing something. As a bike rider on and off since my teens, for some reason or other the Indian Motorcycle marque has eluded me… until recently. Aside from my enjoyment of riding café racers, I had found myself of late sucked into the cruiser world of Harley-Davidson, test riding Sportsters and Low Riders and Sport Glides and Breakouts, and even spending a ton of cash on different machines. But times, and attitudes, change. New Harleys have become extremely expensive, with even second-hand 'bargains' a thing of the past. If you have any in your collection, then they are worth hanging on to.

As I was preparing an article on H-D's 120th anniversary celebrations next year, I read that Indian Motorcycle had come into existence a year earlier, in 1902. The battle for dominance, especially in the US market, had taken hold. Even today in the UK, rivalries exist between bikers. Not violent ones, I hasten to add, but brand loyalties remain strong. It was time for a closer look.

Indian arranged for me to test ride the new FTR R Carbon. I had seen the images, and much appreciated what I saw, but to see the bike in the flesh was a whole different ball game. Changing tenses, it is gorgeous. As Indian explained, the company redefined what an American V-Twin could be with the introduction of its category-defying FTR platform in 2019. And now Indian has taken that platform to a whole new level of street performance with the 2022 FTR line-up. That is not something I

can comment on, because I have nothing to compare the FTR R with from previous iterations, although I appreciate that the bike has been much admired for its unique styling, strong engine and excellent handling – and that I can certainly testify to.

I recently joined around 150 fellow bikers on a Live to Ride event. I rocked up at the start to find Morrisons' car park in Lincoln flooded with all makes, models and ages of bike. As I turned off the engine, I found myself immediately surrounded. "That's lovely," said one biker. "I haven't seen one of those before. Is Indian owned by Harley-Davidson?" Oops. Really?

"Er, no, Indian Motorcycle is owned by Polaris Industries."

"Ah, like the missile?"

"Well, the spelling is the same, and whilst you might consider this bike a missile to ride, it's not exactly on a par with the operational system of four Resolution-class ballistic missile submarines, each armed with 16 Polaris A-3 ballistic missiles. Oh, and they were scrapped by the Royal Navy back in the 1980s."

"Still a lovely bike," he continued, still fuelled by admiration, if somewhat bemused. I was saved from further cross-examination by the sound of engines being fired-up ready for the ride to

LIMITED EDITION 001

Indian

FTR 1200

CARBON R

FTR

Indian

ENGINE: 1203CC, LIQUID-COOLED V-TWIN | **TORQUE:** 87LB-FT/120NM @ 6000RPM | **POWER:** 120HP @ 7750RPM | **FRAME:** STEEL TRELLIS | **FRONT SUSPENSION:** ÖHLINS FULLY ADJUSTABLE INVERTED TELESCOPIC CARTRIDGE FORK | **REAR SUSPENSION:** ÖHLINS FULLY ADJUSTABLE PIGGYBACK IFP | **FRONT BRAKES:** BREMBO DUAL 320MM T5 ROTOR/ FOUR PISTON CALLIPER | **REAR BRAKES:** BREMBO SINGLE 260MM T5 ROTOR/TWO PISTON CALLIPER | **FRONT TYRE:** METZELER SPORTEC 120/70ZR15 58W | **REAR TYRE:** METZELER SPORTEC 180/55ZR17 73W | **EXHAUST:** AKRAPOVIC 2-INTO-1-INTO-2 | **SEAT HEIGHT:** 780MM | **FUEL CAPACITY:** 13 LITRES | **WEIGHT** (EMPTY TANK/FULL OF FUEL): 217KG/232KG | **FACTORY WARRANTY:** TWO YEARS | **STANDARD EQUIPMENT:** RIDE MODES (RAIN, STANDARD, SPORT), LEAN ANGLE SENSITIVE ABS, STABILITY CONTROL, TRACTION CONTROL, WHEELIE CONTROL WITH REAR LIFT MITIGATION, USB CHARGE PORT, CRUISE CONTROL) | **GAUGES:** 4.3 INCH RIDE COMMAND LCD TOUCHSCREEN WITH BLUETOOTH | **CONTACT:** WWW.INDIANMOTORCYCLE.CO.UK

INDIAN HAS TAKEN THE FTR PLATFORM TO A WHOLE NEW LEVEL OF STREET PERFORMANCE WITH THE 2022 FTR LINE-UP

Willingham Woods biker café near Market Rasen, Lincolnshire. Upon arrival, once again the bike acted as a magnet; a metaphor for The North Star or Pole Star – aka Polaris – which is famous for holding nearly still in the sky while the entire northern sky moves around it… in this instance, fellow bikers.

Polaris Industries purchased Indian Motorcycle back in 2011 when it moved operations from North Carolina and merged it into xexisting facilities in Minnesota and Iowa. Since August 2013, the company has marketed multiple modern Indian motorcycles that reflect that company's traditional styling. The quintessentially American brand has continued to go from strength to strength in what remains without doubt a highly competitive industry.

The striking FTR R Carbon brings to the table the flagship model in the FTR line-up, setting itself apart with its glorious carbon fibre tank covers; front fender and headlight nacelle; fully adjustable Öhlins gold front forks and gold piggyback shock; a black Akrapovic exhaust; premium seat cover; and numbered badging on the console.

The FTR R offers a comfortable, upright riding position enhanced by a lower seat height, with those 17 inch wheels combining for a confidence-inspiring, precise ride, with an excellent balance-to-weight ratio and cornering stability, thanks to the Metzeler Sportec tyres and street-tuned suspension.

The 1203cc liquid-cooled V-twin engine produces 120hp and 87lb-ft of torque so you can expect plenty of grunt, even when ridden in the Standard ride mode (there is also Rain and Sport). Nimble in traffic, the bike's penchant is for the open road and would probably be one's weapon of choice for a weekend blast or as a daily commuter. With such a spirited ride on offer, I was surprised there was no quick shifter available as standard equipment, although to be fair it doesn't really need one as the gears are easily flickable, but then the option would be nice.

What's this, a key to turn the bike on? Wasn't expecting that. However, you need that key to open the fuel tank too, so you're not going to lose it. Actually, I found inserting and turning the key to be a bit of a pain as the barrel sits directly behind the 4.7 inch colour touchscreen display. Only a minor niggle.

From the get-go the FTR R offers a smooth, well-calibrated response, with a short first gear offering a fast getaway from traffic lights. Sixth will see you at around 4000rpm at 70mph. Brembos take care of the brakes, with dual 320mm rotors and four-piston callipers at the front and a single 260mm rotor with a two-piston calliper in the rear. I soon grew used to the steadily progressive stopping power, preferring that to over-zealously grabbing a handful of brake because they will bring you up in a hurry faster than you expect.

Another wee gripe is the fuel range. Topped with 3.4 gallons, you can expect around 100 miles of range. Ouch! A tad over 30mpg… at today's prices… But then, if you worry about that, then perhaps you would be better seeking out something that is more pocket friendly.

With its welcome updates for the 2022 model year, the Indian FTR is one part of a family affair, providing a selection of models for different riders throughout a range of price points: the FTR Championship Editor stands at £15,995, FTR Rally at £12,795, FTR S at £14,095, and FTR at £12,295. In addition, Indian Motorcycle is carrying over more than 60 FTR parts and accessories, so you can personalise your bike with a full accessory line ranging from tank covers to high- and low-mount Akrapovic exhaust options; storage bags; a luggage rack; a mid-windshield; and more, obviously depending on which model you opt for.

Talking about price, at a touch over £16,000, is this naked beauty out of everyday reach? That's for you to decide. Apart from a few minor niggles, if you are seeking a planted, engaging ride with oodles of street appeal, then you could do a lot worse than this naked beauty.

Owning an FTR R is tantamount to having a stunning woman on your arm, pretending that showing her off is an everyday occurrence, but knowing deep down you may be punching above your weight. But then, get the right clothes, the right shades, the nonchalant, cool exterior look, and you could possibly get away with it. Win, win. **CRI**

HONDA CMX1100 REBEL DCT

TWIST-AND-GO GO GO

REBEL WITH A CAUSE

WORDS & IMAGES: MICHAEL COWTON

Ridden

Somewhat akin to its namesake Kentucky straight bourbon whiskey, Honda's Rebel is big and bold, and defiantly smooth with a hint of spice… a born classic that will become deservedly famous for its quality. A tad OTT, you ask? Not at all. I have been riding the CMX1100 with six-speed DCT automatic transmission, one of two versions of the new Rebel 1100. DCT is gearing up to be the transmission of the future, and to my mind is the perfect choice for this bike.

There is little wonder that those earlier, smaller displacement Rebel 500 and 300 models became an instant hit with riders both new and experienced. The motors were based on existing sports bike models, and prices were reasonable. Enter the 1100, and Honda has taken things up a notch. I own a couple of Harley cruisers, and recently I had on long-term test a Triumph Speedmaster from the new Bonneville range, but with all due respect, none of them compare to the Rebel in terms of fun and flexibility.

There is definitely something intuitive about this bike, and not once did I sense any lack of control. That is likely due to the 700mm seat height, placing me particularly low to the ground. Add to that the triangular effect of the grips and foot pegs with the seat, not forgetting how light it feels, and everything feels relaxed. And you know what? The odd thing is that I was expecting to keep reaching for the clutch lever, but I didn't… not once.

And that is the beauty of DCT. It is actually a welcoming move away from a manual clutch, although that is still there on the Rebel if you want it, via paddle shifters on the left-hand grip, used simply via thumb and forefinger. First time aboard I flicked the bike to Drive, and it was all twist-and-go. Simple. You see, the dual clutch transmission takes care of the shifting for the rider, so all you have to do is sit back and enjoy the ride. There was only one area where I got flustered a few times, and that was riding at walking pace in heavy traffic at the approach to roundabouts, a time when I like to control a bike's stability by using the rear brake and clutch. It was no big deal though, as at first I just hung back more than usual until I had a relatively safe distance to ride forward.

With throttle-by-wire management, you can play with four preset modes. Sport, naturally, is going to give you a more aggressive feel, maximising power with minimal traction control. Standard is great for pootling around if you're not in a hurry, and I reverted to Rain mode once when I got caught out in a freak burst of the wet stuff, offering the reliance of traction control on any slippery sections. I was riding in early winter, with road debris and leaves clustered in the verges. Thankfully, ABS comes as standard, and remains on all the time. Honda has also treated us to a customisable User mode, where you can choose between three levels of power, traction control and engine braking, and how aggressive you want the shifting to be. I did not get much chance to play with this, but if I get the bike again for a longer test period, it will be fun to use. Nothing like a touch of personalisation.

At first it felt odd that the Rebel popped through the gears with such ease, and upon approaching speed restrictions at villages, I was surprised to see the bike at 30mph and showing fifth! But then, I was sitting over a motor from the Africa Twin, one which has been deliberately detuned for more low rpm power. It is both smooth

HONDA WAS LOOKING TO MARKET AN ENGAGING RIDE, AND ONE WITH ENGINE AND HANDLING PERFORMANCE POTENTIAL TO SPARE

Ridden

Specification

HONDA CMX1100 REBEL DCT | RRP £9999 (£9099 WITHOUT DCT)

ENGINE: 1084CC, LIQUID-COOLED, FOUR-STROKE, EIGHT-VALVE, PARALLEL TWIN | **POWER:** 64KW @ 7000RPM | **TORQUE:** 98NM @ 4750RPM | **TRANSMISSION:** SIX-SPEED | **FRAME:** DIAMOND STEEL | **FRONT SUSPENSION:** PRELOAD ADJUSTABLE 43MM CARTRIDGE STYLE | **REAR SUSPENSION:** PRELOAD ADJUSTABLE TWIN PIGGYBACK REAR SHOCK | **WHEELS:** MULTI-SPOKE CAST ALUMINIUM | **FRONT BRAKE:** RADIAL MOUNTED MONOBLOCK FOUR-PISTON BRAKE CALLIPER, 330MM FLOATING SINGLE DISC | **REAR BRAKE:** TWO SINGLE PISTON CALLIPER, 256MM SINGLE DISC | **FRONT TYRE:** 130/70B18 M/C | **REAR TYRE:** 180/65B16 M/C | **SEAT HEIGHT:** 700MM | **FUEL CAPACITY:** 13.6 LITRES | **GROUND CLEARANCE:** 120MM | **KERB WEIGHT:** 223KG | **CONTACT:** WWW.HONDA.CO.UK

THE BEAUTY OF DCT IS THAT IT IS A WELCOME MOVE AWAY FROM A MANUAL CLUTCH, ALTHOUGH THAT IS STILL THERE IF YOU WANT IT VIA PADDLE SHIFTERS

and satisfying, just like the Rebel bourbon. When it is time to pull up, the Rebel has been treated to a single large 13-inch disc up-front with a radially mounted four-piston Monobloc calliper. At the back end is a 256mm calliper. That rear brake comes in particularly handy in urban environments.

Cornering is a doddle with 43mm cartridge-style front forks, and piggyback rear shocks. A few times I experienced some discomfort on rough roads, but a spanner wrench to the Showa shocks should adjust nicely for a smoother ride.

While chatting with Honda's delivery driver, I was surprised to learn that Honda had been refining and improving DCT for the past eleven years, since the time of the 2010 VFR1200F. Those tweaks are highly impressive, to the point where I thought the bike was reading my mind. If it was, it couldn't rock my mind set, because I always felt wonderfully in control, thanks to the well-balanced chassis and low centre of gravity.

As to the liquid-cooled parallel twin 1084cc engine, while it gives out less than the Africa Twin, you are not going to miss it on this bike because of its size.

I do have a couple of minor niggles, one being the clock display. Sure, there is plenty of information for you to gaze at, but it is all so packed in that it is difficult to pick out some info quickly. Also, I felt that the foot pegs were on the small size, and the side stand looked like an afterthought, too.

The Rebel has a shorter wheelbase than most bikes of this style and is also chain driven as opposed to belt driven like most. And rather than being an out-and-out low-slung cruiser, it sits more comfortably in the sport-cruiser bracket, alongside the likes of the Indian Scout and Kawasaki's Vulcan S.

A quick revisit to the seating position. I'm 6ft with an inside leg of thirty-two inches, and while I enjoy the very low seat, at first I felt somewhat cramped even with the pegs at mid-forward position, as I felt my knees were quite high like a sports bike, but I was surprised at how quickly I bedded myself in and never once felt that I needed a break to stretch my limbs.

While this isn't a touring bike per se, there are various accessories you can acquire to make it your own, by heading down either the Street or the Touring route. The former line-up includes a standard fit diamond stitched – or forward set – replacement seat in black or brown; a rear rack for load

carrying minus the pillion seat; a tank pad; headlight fairing; short front mudguard; and wheel stripes. For that touring look, accessories include replacement rider and pillion comfort seats; passenger back rest and foot pegs; rear rack; fabric saddlebags; and a screen for wind protection. The latter actually offers the bike a completely different look. Swapping my cafe racer hat for that of a cruiser for a moment, that is the way I would probably go with this, as everything will be detachable.

Honda was looking to market an engaging ride, and one with engine and handling performance potential to spare. Without doubt, from the ground up the company has achieved this. Everything about this bike has a nice look and feel. From the blacked-out modern styling to the uncluttered handlebars, this is a bike to be ridden and enjoyed.

And as to the price, expect to pay £9099 without DCT and an additional £900 with DCT. That is, of course, your choice, but whichever you may decide upon, I urge you to ride one. Otherwise, with apologies to David Bowie…

Rebel rebel, how could they know?

Hot tramp, I love you so! **CRI**

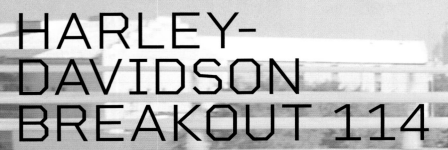

HARLEY-DAVIDSON BREAKOUT 114

BREAKING BAD-ASS

LONG, LEAN, MUSCULAR MACHINE

WORDS: MICHAEL COWTON
IMAGES: HARLEY-DAVIDSON

Ridden

THE BREAKOUT HAS BEEN ON ITS OWN TRAJECTORY, PICKING UP FAN AFTER BADASS FAN ALONG THE WAY

(73kW) @ 5020rpm and a gut-wrenching maximum torque of 161.36Nm (119lb-ft) @ 3000rpm, no punches had been pulled, but then, when you look at the bike, it would be an insult to offer it anything less.

The Breakout started out life in 2013 with a 103cu.in. (1690cc) unit, the same as the Softail Slim which had been introduced the previous year. It was the first Harley to be issued as a CVO model before a standard model was released, and sold out so quickly that Harley then introduced a standard version.

Come 2021, and the Breakout has been on its own trajectory, picking up fan after badass fan along the way.

I managed to secure the loan of a press fleet bike for a week, but sadly did not get that many miles on it because part-way through the week I was away for a couple of days riding the new Pan America across Britain as part of H-D's 'The Great Relay 21'.

When I did happen to be on board, it made my eyes water – literally. The addictive 119lb-ft of torque at my disposal at a mere 3000rpm put one's licence in the danger zone in urban environments, throttle control being a must. This bike is a blast, especially in a straight line. Yes, I know, how many times has that comment been made about Harleys, but the Breakout always has its sights set firmly on the horizon. The rake being set at 34°, you may well want to keep it pointing in an arrow-straight line. And that's without taking into consideration the 240mm wide Michelin Scorcher 11 rear rubber biting the bitumen.

Whilst it remains a difficult pill to swallow, when Harley-Davidson revealed plans for its 'Rewire' strategy (since renamed Hardwire), first announced in April 2020 to replace the 'More Roads to Harley-Davidson' plan put in place in 2018, the need to streamline the product portfolio was always going to be on the cards.

With Covid-19 sweeping the world and H-D facing internal crises with senior staff cuts, and bike sales and revenues enduring a savage beating, the writing was on the wall. A $92 million net loss in the second quarter of 2020 saw the company announce plans to axe up to 30% of its model range.

With Harley's focus on new models, the cuts were going to hit some riders hard, especially when it was announced that the Breakout would disappear alongside other Softail machines, including the Low Rider, Deluxe and the drag-style FXDR 114, which had only hit the market in 2019 but was criticised for its comfort, compromised handling, and with only 5bhp more than the Fat Bob, costing an additional £4000. There was, however, a silver lining for the UK market. While America was to witness the demise of the Breakout, the 2021 model still appeared on the company's UK website.

There are not many bikes that manage to flex their biceps quite like the Breakout; a long, lean, muscular machine housing the mammoth Milwaukee Eight 114 engine and enough drive to power a battleship. With a dry weight of 294kg (648.2lb) and the engine producing a maximum peak output power of 100hp

Specification

HARLEY-DAVIDSON BREAKOUT 114 | RRP FROM £19,995

ENGINE: AIR-COOLED MILWAUKEE EIGHT 114 V-TWIN, 1868CC | **TORQUE:** 155NM @ 3250RPM | **HORSEPOWER:** 94HP/X69KW @ 5020RPM | **CHASSIS:** MILD STEEL TUBULAR FRAME | **RAKE:** 34° | **TRAIL:** 145MM | **SUSPENSION:** 43MM INVERTED FORKS, 130MM TRAVEL, MONOSHOCK REAR END WITH REMOTE PRELOAD ADJUSTMENT, 86MM TRAVEL | **WHEELS:** GASSER II CAST ALUMINIUM (F) 130/60, (R) 240/80 | **BRAKES:** (F) 300MM, FOUR-PISTON FIXED CALLIPER (R) 292MM ROTOR, TWO-PISTON FLOATING CALLIPER, ABS | **TYRES:** MICHELIN SCORCHER II | **FUEL CAPACITY:** 13.2 LITRES | **FUEL ECONOMY:** 43MPG (CLAIMED) | **WET WEIGHT:** 305KG | **SEAT HEIGHT:** 665MM

WHEN IT COMES TO
TIGHTER TURNS, ONCE
YOU COMMIT THAT 21-INCH
FRONT WHEEL TO A LINE
IT'S GOING TO TAKE IT,
NO MATTER WHAT

The last time I did a long road trip it was across Namibia… in a jeep. Nothing but endless miles of gravel and wired fencing to keep roaming cheetahs and leopards at bay. The scenery was spectacular, the weather glorious, my route devoid of traffic. In fact, on one day I passed only four vehicles in a multi-hour stint from Windhoek to the Namib Desert. Parts of America I guess are like that, through Arizona and California and New Mexico; roads disappearing to the horizon, spectacular vistas, prairies and mountains. Makes the heart ache, doesn't it?

But then, of course, you get the sweepies, the winding roads that demand attention, and there are plenty of those around the UK, as we all know. It would be nice to think that that is where the Breakout comes into its own, but of course it doesn't, far from it. It's fine if you are following meandering, almost slalom-like curves, but when it comes to the tighter turns, once you commit that 21-inch front wheel to a line it's going to take it, no matter what. Try and fight it, and you are going to end up arse-sliding into the nearest hedge, so best get it right in the first place. If that means dropping off the revs, then it makes sense. No one wants to throw a bike costing an eye-watering fiver less than £20,000 down the road.

Most testing of all are roundabouts and tight turns, when you have to keep your wits about you, your fingers tickling the clutch and foot on the rear brake to stop tipping over, particularly at slow speeds. Head above 12mph and you can start to breathe easily again… until the next bend, when you need to be aware of the maximum lean angle of this bike… 27 (well, 26.8 actually) degrees. Digging into our human limitations, according to Bernt Spiegel's book, The Upper Half of the Motorcycle, humans have developed an internal programme that allows us to lean a motorcycle, albeit only to a certain point, that being pre-set at 20°. Fortunately, we can exceed our natural capacity by gaining a better sense of stability, and that comes from practise. Watching MotoGP riders scraping knee sliders at over 50° puts the fear of God in many of us, and merely the sound of a Harley foot peg scraping on Tarmac is enough to jolt us upright, but once you get used to it, it is nothing to fear – you just know that you have hit your, or the bike's, limit. So, remember to look for the limit point, pick your line, and take the corner at a sensible speed before powering out, making full use of that M8 engine.

What I particularly like is the fact that if you want to sit back and enjoy the ride without inducing any hairs-on-the-back-of-the-neck thrill, the Breakout is wonderfully versatile, happily sitting at or below 2000rpm, even in a high gear.

In conclusion then, there are plenty of good reasons to buy a Breakout. I am not sure whether I would have one as my main ride, but as a missile to hoon around on at weekends, there is not much to compete with it. And should you have the money for a new model to hand over to your dealer, bear in mind that like most other models in the Harley range, resale values hold firm. A few years back I noted that H-D bikes retained an average of 84% of their value over a five-year period… so there you go, five years of being an utter badass hooligan. **CRI**

AS A MISSILE TO HOON AROUND ON AT WEEKENDS, THERE IS NOT MUCH TO COMPETE WITH IT

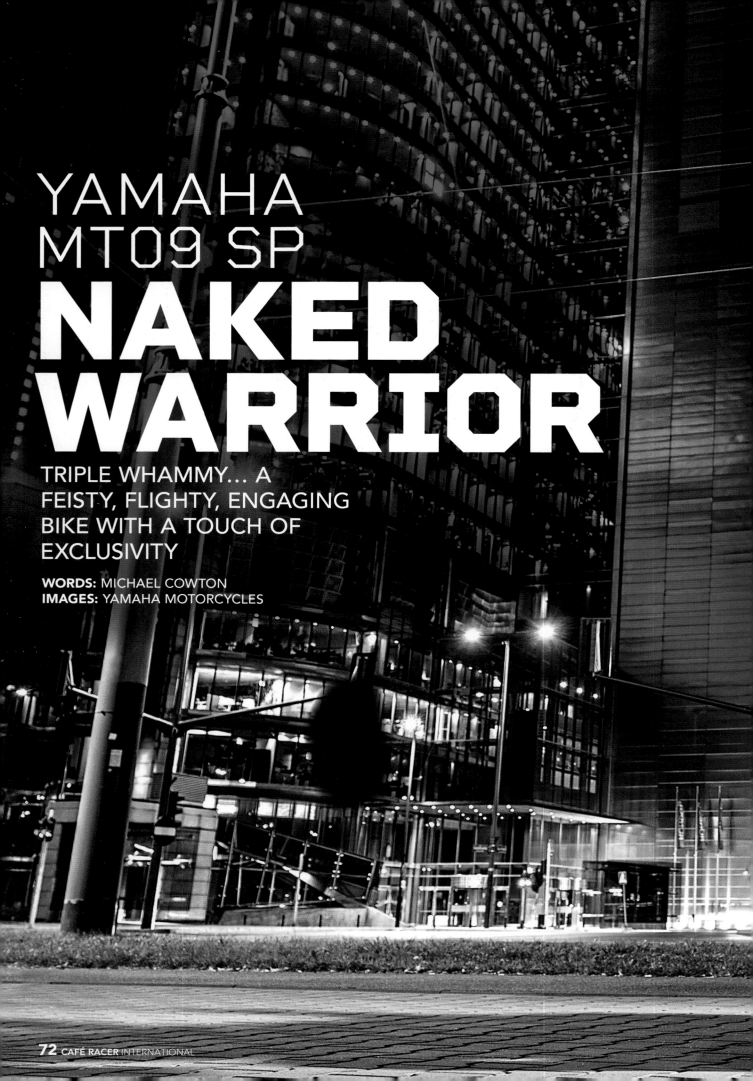

YAMAHA MT09 SP

NAKED WARRIOR

TRIPLE WHAMMY... A FEISTY, FLIGHTY, ENGAGING BIKE WITH A TOUCH OF EXCLUSIVITY

WORDS: MICHAEL COWTON
IMAGES: YAMAHA MOTORCYCLES

t's extraordinary how time flies. It's been nine years – yes, nine years – since the engineers at Yamaha first unveiled the MT-09. Standing naked to the world, there was little surprise how well it took off with its engaging looks, linear torque and incredible agility. Fast-forward almost a decade, and the MT-09 marches on, growing in range and stature, along the way adding a touch of exclusivity with the SP model.

Like a Stormtrooper in jack boots, it kicked many rivals into touch on its march to prominence. The top dogs at Yamaha clearly knew they were on to a winner. To introduce my somewhat limited knowledge of linguistics, a collocation is the habitual juxtaposition of a particular word with another word or words with a frequency greater than chance. Glad I got that out of the way. Living legend, that's a collocation, and I'll use it here, because that's what the venerable MT-09 is. And it's even grander in SP format.

A 2021 MT-09 revision took place due to Euro 5 engine compliancy. Revision? Perhaps overhaul or renovation would be a better word, as the SP version took things a stage further with the addition of a gold-coloured Öhlins rear shock; upgraded KYB forks; polished swingarm; double stitching on the seat; cruise control; and YZF-R1M-inspired tricolor scheme. It looks gorgeous. It sounds gorgeous. It rides beautifully. Whilst not in the literal sense, it's got exclusivity stamped all over it. That's why the price for an MT-09 iteration has crept over the £10k price tag for the very first time.

Competition-wise, the MT-09 sits proudly in the starting blocks alongside the Kawasaki Z900, Triumph Street Triple and the Agusta Brutale 800; streetfighters all, with the Yamaha's inline-three engine offering the power of three: power, torque and low weight. In fact, the MT-09 with its 890cc engine is the first Yamaha bike since the days of the XS750 and XS850 to be powered by an in-line power unit.

I admit to being a fan of cruise control, particularly as it adds versatility and relaxation, not only on long rides, but also urban outings and daily commutes. On the SP it's smoothly functional, offering single mph increments via the toggle switch on the left-hand side of the handlebar. Like other bikes, cancellation is done by a pull of the clutch lever or dab of the brake, provided the transmission is in fourth gear or higher and speed is no less than 31mph. Comfort comes via the carbon-coated KYB fork which is adjustable for separate high- and low-speed compression damping, as well as rebound damping and spring preload. While the quickshifter is now working both up and down, gear changes remain wonderfully smooth

I was certainly impressed by the spread of useable torque, making it effortless to trundle through towns and villages, with a twist of the throttle powering me to the national speed limit within the blink of an eye. Accelerating from bends and power overtakes are simplicity itself, thanks to the mid-range torque. A peak figure of 68.6lb-ft (93Nm) is found at 7000rpm.

The SP is equipped with a 3.5in full-colour TFT display featuring a bar-type tachometer that changes colour as rpm rises or falls; plus a clock and displays for what's left in the tank; average mileage; water temperature; air temperature and a gearshift indicator – all easily switchable between displays and information via the handlebar switches.

For night-time riding, the bike benefits from a bifunctional (low and high beam in one) LED headlight which offers a wide beam spread. Instead of the conventional 'mono-focus' type headlight, the MT-09 SP utilises a projector design with a built-in internal lens in addition to the thick outer lens. The turn signals and newly-designed tail light are also LED.

And while I wax lyrical about this super-beast of a bike, let's not forget that the MT journey continues with the updated 2022 MT-10 – a bigger, more powerful, nutty bike if that grabs you. While the MT-07 remains the best-seller, if you want a big bang for your buck, then sit astride the missile that is the MT-09 SP and light the touchpaper. You have been warned. **CRI**

Specification

YAMAHA MT-09 SP | PRICE: £10,202

ENGINE: 889CC, THREE CYLINDER, LIQUID-COOLED, FOUR-STROKE, FOUR VALVES, DOHC | **POWER:** 117.4BHP/87.5KW @ 10,000RPM | **TORQUE:** 68.6LB-FT (93NM) @ 7000RPM | **TRANSMISSION:** SIX SPEED | **FRAME:** DIAMOND STYLE WITH CRYSTAL GRAPHITE FINISH | **FRONT SUSPENSION:** KYB 41MM TELESCOPIC FORKS, 130MM TRAVEL | **REAR SUSPENSION:** SWING ARM (LINK SUSPENSION) OHLINS REAR SHOCK, 122MM TRAVEL | **FRONT BRAKE:** HYDRAULIC DUAL DISC | **REAR BRAKE:** HYDRAULIC SINGLE DISC | **WHEELS:** TUBELESS, ALUMINIUM | **FRONT TYRE:** BRIDGESTONE S22, 120/70 ZR17M/C (58W) | **REAR TYRE:** BRIDGESTONE S22, 180/55 ZR17M/C (73W) | **WEIGHT:** 189KG | **SEAT HEIGHT:** 825MM | **FUEL CAPACITY:** 14 LITRES | **FUEL CONSUMPTION:** 56.5MPG (CLAIMED) | **WARRANTY:** TWO YEARS / UNLIMITED MILES | **CONTACT:** YAMAHA-MOTOR.EU

YAMAHA
MT-07

YAMAHA HAS SOLD IN EXCESS OF 125,000 UNITS, SO CLEARLY IT HAS BEEN DOING SOMETHING RIGHT

WORDS: MICHAEL COWTON
IMAGES: YAMAHA MOTORCYCLES

Ridden

There are some bikes that are all things to all men and women, of all ages and abilities. The MT-07 is one such machine. As an all-rounder it is second-to-none, which is why it remains the best-seller in the MT line-up. Well, that and the price tag.

Having made its debut seven years ago, the itch remains to ride one. That'll be in part due to its aggressive, naked styling, punchy engine and lightweight, effortless ride quality. Its multi-purposefulness comes into play, too. I have seen plenty of newly-qualified riders on one. I know people who use one as a commuter, and others for simply having fun on at a weekend.

So, what does it sit alongside? The Suzuki CB650R, Kawasaki's Ninja 650, and one I rode and enjoyed recently – Triumph's Trident 660, for sure, as others have been quick to identify. To my mind, the SP-07 rises to the challenge in the agility stakes, with rider engagement to the fore.

The bike comes fitted with full LED lights in a Y-shaped icon, adding to its striking good looks. And while it has a muscular, aggressive stance and is no pussycat, it's easy to get on with and is happy to do everything you ask of it – within reason. New riders on a restricted MT-07 will enjoy its low-speed manoeuvrability, and while I admit to being crap at U-turns having dropped a bike recently (not the MT-07, and probably not looking in the right direction at the time!), this bike is so user-friendly I love it for its forgiving nature. Look after it, and it will look after you, for sure.

The riding position of the punchy 689cc parallel twin is extremely comfortable, even after a few hours in the saddle, although taller riders than me (I'm 6ft), might find the legs get a bit cramped due to the position of the pegs. The bike has been tweaked to comply with the latest Euro 5 regs, but that has certainly not compromised its performance. Throttle response is impressive, without being snatchy, and the rubber front and rear stick to the road like glue as you ride into the hairiest of corners. With the same frame and suspension set up from the 2018 update, the dual front discs have increased in size from 282mm to 298mm, so throwing out the anchors makes for a less heart-pumping experience.

Honda has sold in excess of 125,000 units, so clearly it has been doing something right over the past eight years since the MT-07 first hit the street in 2014. It's difficult, if not impossible, not to like the hyper naked, and the 2022 iteration comes with new bodywork including twin winglet-type air intakes and that compact LED headlight with its standalone Y-shape face. This big seller in the middleweight class now boasts wider aluminium taper handlebars, making turning so much easier and compliant. And don't let's forget the tweaked engine to meet those Euro5 emissions compliancy.

The MT-07 is a born entertainer – engaging, fun, and characterful, plus cheap as chips for what is on offer. Whether you are a novice rider, or a seasoned old pro who wants to downsize and knock a few kilos off the weight (the bike), then it's definitely worth a second, or even third, glance. **CRI**

Specification

YAMAHA MT-07 | PRICE: £6899

ENGINE: 689CC FOUR VALVE, DOHC LIQUID-COOLED PARALLEL TWIN | **POWER:** 74BHP @ 9000RPM | **TORQUE:** 68NM @ 6500RPM | **TRANSMISSION:** SIX SPEED | **FRAME:** DIAMOND | **FRONT SUSPENSION:** CONVENTIONAL FORKS, NON-ADJUSTABLE | **REAR SUSPENSION:** SINGLE SHOCK, PRELOAD AND REBOUND ADJUSTABLE | **FRONT BRAKE:** DUAL FOUR-PISTON CALLIPERS, 298MM DISCS, ABS | **REAR BRAKE:** SINGLE-PISTON CALLIPER, 245MM DISC, ABS | **FRONT TYRE:** 120/70 X 17 | **REAR TYRE:** 180/55 X 17 | **ABS:** YES | **TRACTION CONTROL:** YES | **FUEL CAPACITY:** 14 LITRES (3.7 GALLONS) | **FUEL CONSUMPTION:** 51MPG (CLAIMED) | **WEIGHT:** 189KG | **SEAT HEIGHT:** 825MM (32.5 IN) | **WARRANTY:** TWO YEARS | **CONTACT:** YAMAHA-MOTOR.EU

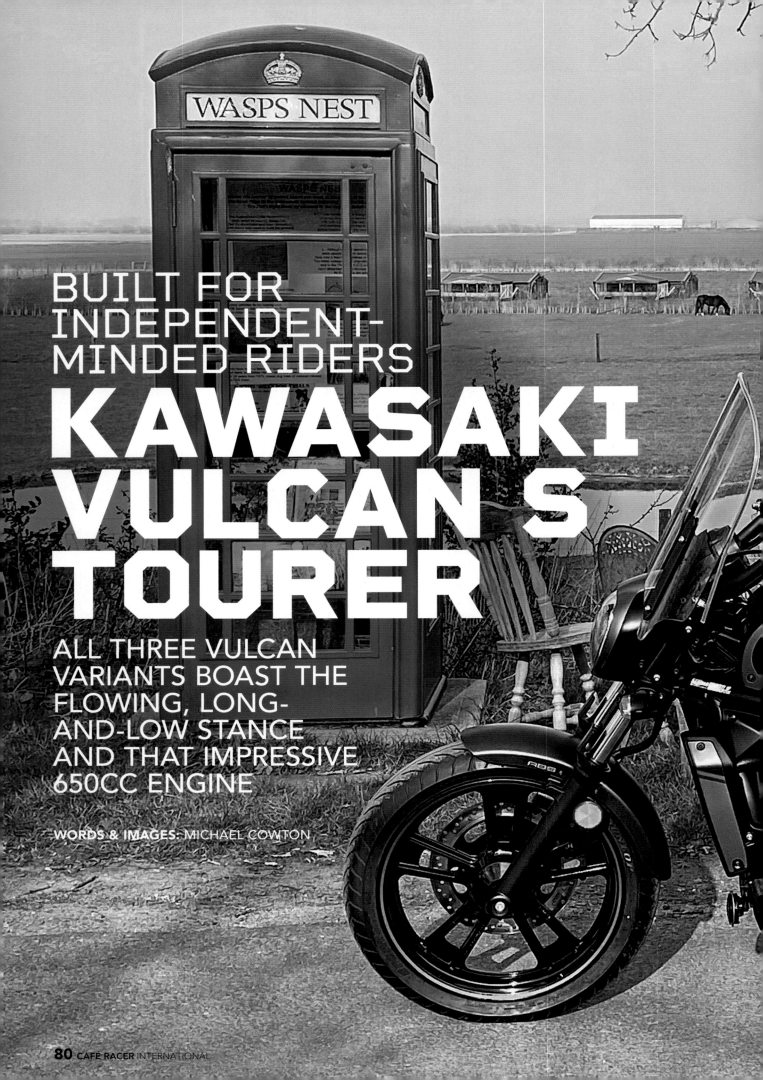

BUILT FOR
INDEPENDENT-
MINDED RIDERS

KAWASAKI VULCAN S TOURER

ALL THREE VULCAN
VARIANTS BOAST THE
FLOWING, LONG-
AND-LOW STANCE
AND THAT IMPRESSIVE
650CC ENGINE

WORDS & IMAGES: MICHAEL COWTON

Am I going Kwakers, you may well ask? A tourer in a café racer magazine! Sacrilege or what! Not really because, you see, Kawasaki's Vulcan S Tourer is not your average cruiser. For a start it doesn't conform to any type of herd mentality, any trend however outdated or, indeed, lifestyle for that matter. Designed for independent-minded riders, it is perfectly capable of standing apart from the crowd with its parallel twin engine, unique frame and suspension layout.

Its versatility comes about with the addition of luggage panniers and added wind protection from a large screen, so if you want to switch from a pleasant day ride to an overnighter, no problem. It also offers an excellent riding platform, with its compact engine and slim frame resulting in a design that is narrow at the knees and feet. There's no need to tuck those knees under your chin either, giving yourself cramp after a long ride, because the forward-positioned foot pegs are perfect for relaxed, cruiser-style riding.

There I go again… cruiser. I'm getting to that age where I like a change of ride occasionally, and the sculpted design and thick padding offered on the Vulcan S offer both excellent comfort and good hip support. So yes, whilst I love café racers and am always happy to throw my leg over a Royal Enfield Continental GT or the glorious Triumph Thruxton, there's nothing wrong with having a few options in the garage, depending on your mood for the day.

I rode it both with and without the windshield, and removing the panniers gave it a completely different look. I would say wind protection is adequate with the screen in situ, but having spent a couple of minutes removing it by four bolts, sans windshield, the 'naked' look is a winner, giving the bike an even more non-conventional look, with more of the wind blast hitting you in the torso as opposed to round the helmet, a bonus to my mind. But the mere fact of having those two large luggage panniers available to drop in camera, waterproofs, and anything else you might need – rather than having to carry a rucksack or belt pack – is a bonus.

The Vulcan comes in three variants, the Standard, Tourer and Performance. They all boast the flowing, long-and-low stance and that impressive 650cc engine. My first thought was whether

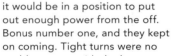

it would be in a position to put out enough power from the off. Bonus number one, and they kept on coming. Tight turns were no problem, even with the low centre of gravity. I didn't manage to scrape the pegs, but I'm sure I wasn't far off on occasion.

Torque was impressive throughout the range, and that parallel-twin liquid-cooled engine offered up hardly any vibration, so on longer rides it was always comfort first and foremost. Interestingly, while there is plenty of power from the lower rpm range, wind it up above 5000rpm and the bike takes on a new persona, not quite café racer, but not far off. Extraordinary. Yep, this bike definitely has attitude, even if it looks considerably chilled on its side stand.

The ABS-controlled braking comes via a single 300mm disc up-front with a twin-piston calliper, and the rear is taken care of by a single 250mm disc with a single-piston calliper.

It is clear that the Vulcan was built to inspire confidence across the riding spectrum, offering a smooth take-up from the start, and a satisfyingly smooth acceleration. Twist that throttle and traffic merging and overtaking is no problem.

The instrumentation cluster features an easy-to-read analogue-style tachometer and multi-purpose LCD. Other features include a 14-litre fuel tank capacity and good fuel economy, meaning those long rangers amongst you can go longer between fuel stops, a reassuring quality when on day trips.

Star Trekkies will know of the Vulcans as the fictional extra-terrestrial humanoid species, noted for their attempt to live by logic and reason with as little interference from emotion as possible. I reckon the Vulcan S Tourer resides in the same parallel universe. It doesn't brag or boast about its looks or power and agility, quietly confident that once you ride it, you get it. At the time of writing, I was waiting for a call from Kawasaki for the return of the bike. I might just take the phone off the hook… **CRI**

Specification

KAWASAKI VULCAN S TOURER | **PRICE:** (starting from) **£7489**
ENGINE: LIQUID-COOLED, FOUR-STROKE PARALLEL TWIN | **POWER:** 44.7KW {61PS} @ 7500RPM | **TORQUE:** 62.4NM @ 6600RPM | **TRANSMISSION:** SIX-SPEED | **FRAME:** TUBULAR DIAMOND, HIGH-TENSILE STEEL | **FINAL DRIVE:** SEALED CHAIN | **FRONT BRAKE:** SINGLE 300MM DISC, CALLIPER, DUAL-PISTON | **REAR BRAKE:** SINGLE 250MM, CALLIPER, SINGLE-PISTON | **FRONT SUSPENSION:** 41MM TELESCOPIC FORK | **REAR SUSPENSION:** OFFSET LAYDOWN SINGLE-SHOCK, LINKAGE EQUIPPED, WITH SEVEN-WAY ADJUSTABLE PRELOAD | **FRONT TYRE:** 120/70 R18M/C 59H | **REAR TYRE:** 160/60 717M/C 69H | **GROUND CLEARANCE:** 123MM | **FUEL CAPACITY:** 14 LITRES | **SEAT HEIGHT:** 705MM | **WEIGHT:** 229KG | **CONTACT:** KAWASAKI.CO.UK

MUSCLE AND
MASCULINITY

HARLEY-DAVIDSON FAT BOB 114

MODESTLY
UNDERSTATED, THIS
BIKE IS BREAKING
NEW GROUND

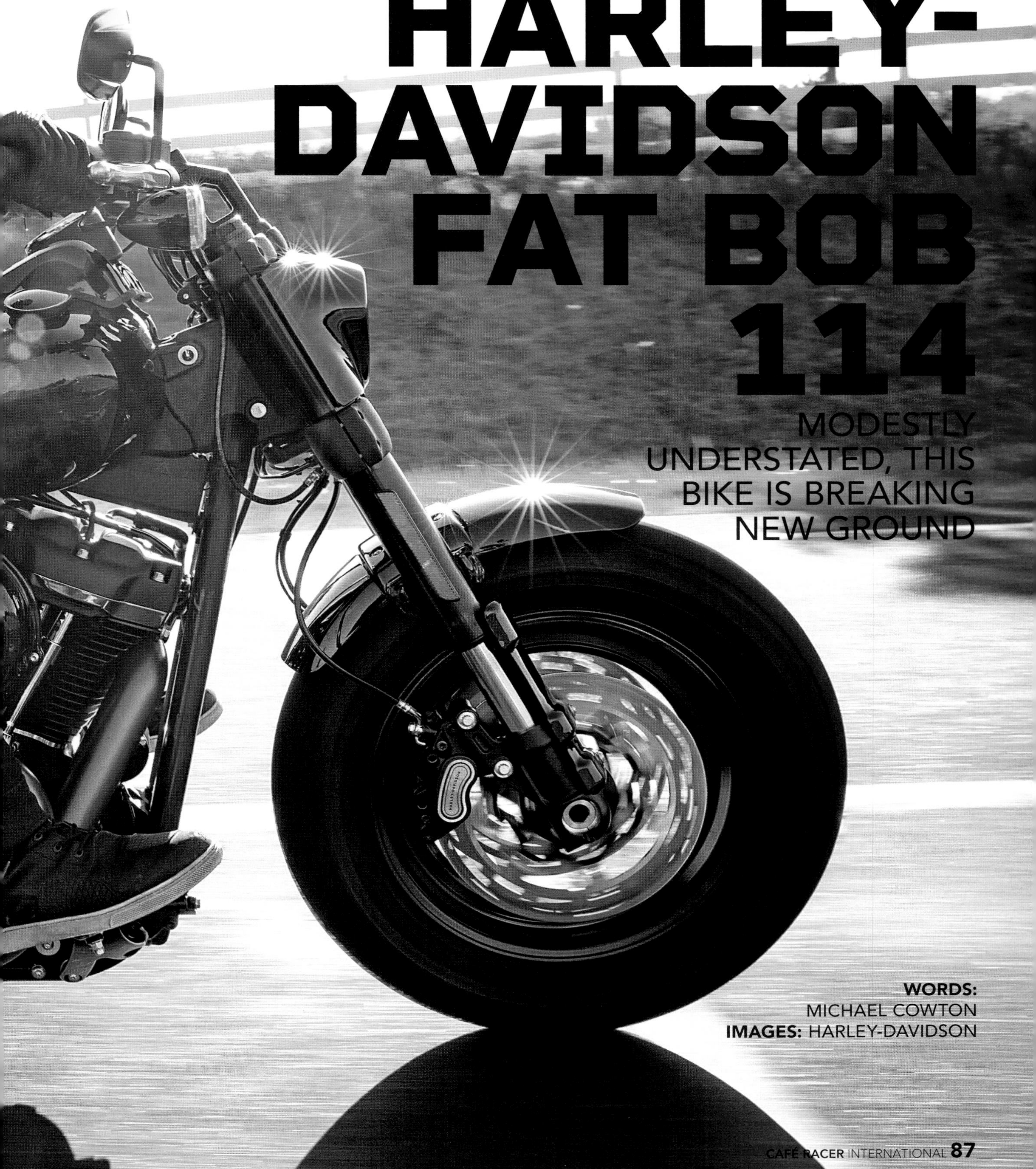

WORDS:
MICHAEL COWTON
IMAGES: HARLEY-DAVIDSON

WITHOUT DOUBT THIS IS A SHOWPIECE BIKE, ONE THAT CAN HUSTLE WITH THE BEST OF THEM, BUT ONE DEVOID OF MODERN GIZMOS, SO DON'T EXPECT BUNDLES OF RIDER MODES

AS the decade of elegance and glamour, the 1930s had ridden in on the coattails of the decadent 1920s jazz age, a period when women had cut their hair and dressed like boys. Attitude was everything, alongside style and influence, and the backlash was unleashed. Women then looked towards Hollywood, became feminine once again and abandoned trousers suits, turned into dizzy blondes and took to wearing silk, velvet and fur. The Second World War put paid to that, leaving little money to frizzle away on clothes and recycling old material came into its own.

In order to read the market, one needs to research, analyse and gain insight before trends can take hold. As the jazz age had taken a hold, so, too, in the 1920s did a new trend in the world of motorbikes, one that would continue well into the 1990s thanks to 'bob-job', the original name of the bobber custom motorcycle. Stripped of excess bodywork, with the front fender gone, the rear fender shortened (bobbed), and any other superfluous parts discarded to save weight. Stripped and ready for action.

The release of Harley-Davidson's 'J' Series V-Twin saw creativity take a hold as home builders took their stock bikes and went down the modification route with a lowered bike with small diameter wheels, a cut-down frame and shorter rear section, all directed towards a solo rider.

The distinctive shape identified by the sweeping diagonal line between the steering head and rear axle could not be mistaken. Bob-job was born. Other bikers quickly took note and the 'California Cut-Down' phase began. Come the 1930s, and both H-D and Indian were producing bikes that followed the cut-down trend. Even racers determined to increase performance began discarding the front fender and creating a 'bob-tail' rear fender. Bob-job was born.

I was recently watching a television documentary on movie icon Marlon Brando, famed for his role in The Wild One. While Brando chose to ride his own Triumph Thunderbird in the film, his nemesis in the film, Lee Marvin, sat astride a bobber-style Harley Panhead.

Manufacturer modifications continued as more and more accessories appeared on the shelves to further enhance

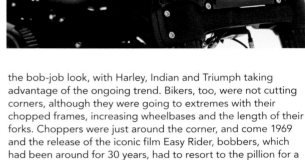

the bob-job look, with Harley, Indian and Triumph taking advantage of the ongoing trend. Bikers, too, were not cutting corners, although they were going to extremes with their chopped frames, increasing wheelbases and the length of their forks. Choppers were just around the corner, and come 1969 and the release of the iconic film Easy Rider, bobbers, which had been around for 30 years, had to resort to the pillion for a while (yes, I know traditionally there isn't one on a bobber!).

Whilst many back-shed bike builders turned their attention to the growing trend in café racers, bobbers were by no means dead in the water. Come the new millennium, and the custom scene was re-emerging. In Britain, Triumph brought back the ever-popular Bonneville, yet another platform ripe for customisation, and in today's family line-up, introduced in 2021, the Triumph Bobber is one of the marque's best-selling bikes. A simple mod by adding a small pillion seat and you also have the fast-selling Speedmaster.

And so to Harley, whose Street Bob has undergone several transitions since its debut in the Dyna series in 2006 through to 2016, when a change was made from the Twin Cam 96 to the Twin Cam 103 in 2014. Three years later, the Street Bob became a Softail and acquired the Milwaukee-Eight 107 powerplant. The latest, 2021 iteration remains the lightest Softail model yet to use the Milwaukee-Eight 114 engine. With 90 horses and 119lb-ft of torque, you can expect its bark to be backed up with plenty of bite.

Aside from the popular new Street Bob, to my mind of the current cache of bikes on the market, Harley's revamped Fat Bob remains the most striking of the bunch, so named after its blend of broad gas tank and cut-down bobber style… yes, that word 'style' again, as opposed to a type of motorcycle. The Fat Bob certainly benefitted from emerging from the Dyna into the Softail line-up in 2018, enhanced by a different frame, swing arm, suspension and rubbed-mounted engine.

Specification

HARLEY FAT BOB 114 |
PRICE: £16,995 (VIVID BLACK),
ADD £350 FOR VIVID RED OR
DEADWOOD GREEN DENIM
ENGINE: MILWAUKEE-EIGHT 114 V-TWIN | **POWER:**
93HP/69KW @ 5020RPM | **TORQUE:** 155NM/118LB-FT @
3500RPM | **WHEELBASE:** 1615MM | **BRAKES:** CALLIPER
TYPE, FOUR-PISTON FIXED FRONT AND TWO-PISTON
FLOATING REAR | **TRANSMISSION:** SIX-SPEED |
SUSPENSION: (F) NON-ADJUSTABLE 43MM INVERTED
CARTRIDGE FORK WITH TRIPLE-RATE SPRINGS; 5.1
INCHES (R) SPRING-PRELOAD ADJUSTABLE SHOCK; 4.4
INCHES | **WHEELS:** (F) AND (R) DENIM BLACK, CAST
ALUMINIUM WITH LASER ETCHED GRAPHICS |
TYRES: (F) 150/80 x 16 (R) 180/70 x 16 | **SEAT HEIGHT:**
28 INCHES | **FUEL CAPACITY:** 3.6 GALLONS |
ESTIMATED FUEL ECONOMY: 43MPG | **WEIGHT:**
306KG | **CONTACT:** HARLEY-DAVIDSON.COM

ASIDE FROM THE POPULAR NEW STREET BOB, TO MY MIND OF THE CURRENT CACHE OF BIKES ON THE MARKET, HARLEY'S REVAMPED FAT BOB REMAINS THE MOST STRIKING OF THE BUNCH

Ridden

When I drew up at a local café the Fat Bob was immediately surrounded by bikers, some from the local H-D Chapter. For some it was the first time they had seen one, and proved to be a star in its own right; with its cool, yet muscular, street-style expressionism, fat tyres, understated paint scheme and stubby appearance. Harley has been very clever here, because the Fat Bob oozes presence; it draws you in to take a closer look, tempting you to crawl on to its back.

That squatness soon disappears as you straddle the 28in high seat, take hold of the drag bars and lift the 675lb bike off its side stand. I rode out ahead of a friend on his Honda CBR600. After a pleasant ride along some long straights and sweeping country roads, he commented that he had never seen anyone carve so easily on a Harley. Let me assure you that that was not me, but the bike offering such an amazingly confidence-inspiring ride. I was pleasantly surprised at how easily it flicked into corners for a machine of its size, and not once did I feel unstable, the brakes offering excellent bite when needed. It was almost as if this bike had been specially engineered for Britain's bends, with enough traction to spare to appease even the twitchiest of riders.

If it's muscle and masculinity you are seeking, then the Fat Bob should flex your desires. Even in urban sprawl it's a doddle to ride, versatility being one of its key strengths. Talking about strength, bear in mind that if you go for this latest iteration, it only comes available with the stonking Milwaukee-Eight 114 powerplant. And what about humps and bumps? Nah. Harley has taken care of that, too, with a 43mm inverted fork offering over five inches of travel, and the rear offering 4.4 inches nicely taming the tarmac.

I guess what is most striking about the Fat Bob is those upswept dual exhaust cans and the exhaust cover with its neat copper patina beautifully set against the blacked-out engine, topped off with fat tyres. This being of the bobber style, the pillion seat is small, tiny even, although the foot pegs are positioned such that the rider can make use of them for a change, offering a completely different, almost sporty, riding stance.

So, without doubt this is a showpiece bike, one that can hustle with the best of them, but one devoid of modern gizmos – so don't expect bundles of rider modes. You do get ABS, and you can change the trip counter, but that's about it, although there is an analogue tachometer with digital speedometer; gear indicator (always useful); odometer; fuel level; clock; trip and range indication.

But then this bike is not about gimmicks, it's a rider's bike, as all Harleys are. It's extremely comfortable and, if modestly understated, it's breaking new ground. And while it stands naked against some of the marque's other big bruisers, it still takes some manoeuvring in tight spots. Well, it is Harley, after all, and a bloody good one at that. **CRI**

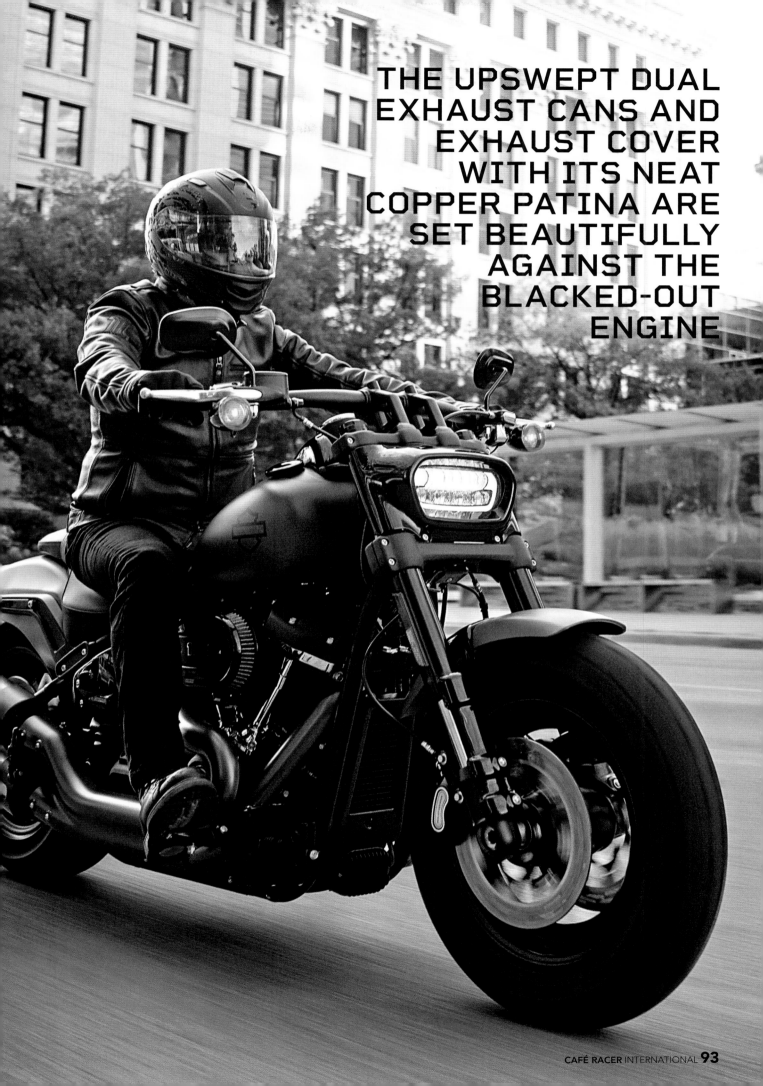

THE UPSWEPT DUAL
EXHAUST CANS AND
EXHAUST COVER
WITH ITS NEAT
COPPER PATINA ARE
SET BEAUTIFULLY
AGAINST THE
BLACKED-OUT
ENGINE

BACK TO THE FUTURE
KAWASAKI
Z650RS

BUILDING ON THE SUCCESS OF ITS Z900RS,
KAWASAKI DECIDED TO GIVE ITS Z650 A
RETRO-THEMED REBOOT, TOO

WORDS: ROSS MOWBRAY **IMAGES:** KAWASAKI EUROPE

Taking styling inspiration from the 1977 B1 Z650, 'classic' bike fanatics will no doubt baulk at any comparison between Kawasaki's four-cylinder icon and its newest namesake, but you cannot blame the Japanese factory for making something of its heritage, even if the Z650RS is essentially a Z650 with a stylish new frock.

That is no bad thing by the way. The Z650 is a cracking bike, being light, agile and easy to ride with plenty of punch to put a smile on your face. Add a round LED headlight, a chunky fuel tank and a duck-style rear end into the mix and you have got the new Z650RS.

The bike shares plenty with the 'standard' Z650. Its engine, chassis, brakes and suspension are all pretty much identical to the naked sports bike, but there are some subtle changes that help make it stand out.

The engine is the same as the latest generation Z650 with performance levels to match. That means there is peak power of 67.3bhp available at 8000rpm and 47.2lb-ft of peak torque

at 6700rpm. Those figures are not really anything to write home about, but they do stand up against the current crop of middleweight retro motorcycles (and even most of the similar-sized nakeds, too). It is a lovely motor with plenty of punch available right through the rev range.

Kawasaki says it's been tuned for a more plentiful supply of power in the low and mid-range, but it's by no means asthmatic up top. It is a joy to ride in town, rolling on and off in second as I nipped through the rush-hour traffic in Marseille. It was even better on the twisty roads above the French city, offering a rewarding ride soundtracked by the glorious noise from the stylish standard exhaust. It will happily barrel along at motorway speeds, too, with enough in reserve to make higher speed overtakes a breeze.

Fitting with its retro outlook, simplicity is the name of the game. There are no rider modes, cornering ABS settings or wheelie controls to mess about with. It is a simple, back-to-basics motorcycle with no faff and it works very well.

As a quick aside, Kawasaki reckons the Z650RS is the perfect weapon for learner riders who are working their way up through the licence categories. As such, it is offering the option to add a dealer-fit restriction kit which will taper down performance to an A2-legal 35kW.

Ridden

Specification

KAWASAKI Z650RS | **RRP** FROM **£7549**
ENGINE: 649CC FOUR-STROKE LIQUID-COOLED PARALLEL TWIN, DOHC, EIGHT VALVES | **POWER:** 50.2KW / 67.3BHP @ 8000RPM (A2 RESTRICTED VERSION: 35KW / 47BHP) | **TORQUE:** 64NM/47.2LB-FT @ 6700RPM (A2 RESTRICTED VERSION: 58NM / 42.7LB-FT) | **TRANSMISSION:** SIX-SPEED, SEALED CHAIN DRIVE | **FRAME:** TRELLIS, HIGH-TENSILE STEEL | **SUSPENSION:** (F) 41MM TELESCOPIC FORKS, 125MM TRAVEL (R) HORIZONTAL BACKLINK, 130MM TRAVEL AND PRE-LOAD ADJUSTMENT | **BRAKES:** (F) DUAL SEMI-FLOATING 300MM DISCS, DUAL PISTON NISSIN CALLIPER (R) SINGLE 220MM DISC, SINGLE NISSIN CALLIPER | **WHEELS/TYRES:** (F) 120/70 ZR17 DUNLOP SPORTMAX ROADSPORT 2 (R) 160/60 ZR17 DUNLOP SPORTMAX ROADSPORT 2 | **SEAT HEIGHT:** 820MM | **WEIGHT:** 187KG (WET) | **FUEL CAPACITY:** 12 LITRES (2.6 GALLONS) | **FUEL CONSUMPTION:** CLAIMED: 62.7MPG (4.5L / 100KM) / TESTED: 52.1MPG (5.2L / 100KM) | **WARRANTY:** TWO YEARS, UNLIMITED MILES (WITH THE OPTION TO EXTEND) | **SERVICING:** 600 MILES/7000 MILES OR ONE YEAR | **CONTACT:** WWW.KAWASAKI.CO.UK

YOU WOULD BE
WRONG TO THINK
THAT THE RETRO Z650
PRIORITISES STYLE
OVER SUBSTANCE

FOR AN AN EASY-TO-RIDE, STYLISH MOTORCYCLE THAT IS HAPPY CUTTING THROUGH TRAFFIC AND BEING PUSHED HARD ON THE OPEN ROAD, THEN THE Z650RS IS WORTH A LOOK

The six-speed gearbox is slick enough with a reassuring click as you snick up and down the box, and although there is no quick-shifter available, it is unlikely you will ever think about needing one. Aggressive down changes on the approach to sharp corners did cause things to get a bit squirrelly at the rear on a couple of occasions, but that was probably more down to the wet roads than any issue with the bike.

The Z650RS gets a 12-litre fuel tank, and with a claimed 62.7mpg, Kawasaki reckons you should be able to cover 150 miles without needing to top up. If you are riding hard on faster roads that figure is going to drop down a fraction. At the end of a day of spirited riding I had managed to knock that down to 52.1mpg (which means you should still have no trouble managing 130 miles from a full tank).

The suspension is not the most sophisticated. That said, the 41mm conventional forks up front do their job well enough, with little dive under aggressive braking, while at the rear the horizontal monoshock with pre-load adjustment seems to offer a decent compromise between comfort and performance. You will not be adjusting it on the fly though, as it is tucked away under

the seat and does not look the easiest to get at, so once you have set it up, you will likely want to leave it be.

The brakes are up to the job, too. At the front twin-pot Nissin callipers grab a pair of round 300mm discs (in place of the petal-style numbers on the standard Z650), while at the rear a single 220mm disc is on hand to help with stopping. There is plenty of feel from the span-adjustable lever for when you want to keep things a bit more delicate, but when you need to slow down in a hurry, rest assured that there is plenty of bite. There is also plenty of engine braking if you knock it down a gear on the way into corners. I like that.

The chassis is particularly good. You would be wrong to think that the retro Z650 prioritises style over substance. The handling is light and agile, with the wide bars making it easy to muscle the bike through tight turns and bob and weave around in congested city traffic. The cast spoked wheels are shod with a set of Dunlop Sportmax Roadsport 2 rubber which more than held their own on cold, damp tarmac before being pressed harder when things dried out in the afternoon.

The seat is not as plush as I had expected, but there is plenty of padding, so I suspect it would give a little bit over time. It stands at a manageable 820mm tall, but shorter riders need not worry as there is an 800mm low seat option. I am 6ft 1in tall, and although it was not the roomiest of rides (thanks in part to the high foot pegs to aid ground clearance), I did not have any aches or pains after a full day in the saddle.

If you are in the market for an easy-to-ride, stylish motorcycle that is happy cutting through traffic and being pushed hard on the open road, then the Z650RS is worth a look. Kawasaki is expecting that it will be particularly popular with the younger, less experienced and more style-conscious of us (which is why there is that A2 restrictor kit available from affiliated dealers), but it also reckons it will do well with older riders who remember the original bike from back in the day.

There is a hell of a lot of competition out there though, with a bike to suit every budget. The closest is probably Yamaha's XSR700 (which is £150 more expensive). Kawasaki is still feeling optimistic about how well it is going to go down in the UK. It has ordered more of them than it has standard Z650s and Ninja 650s. We like the confidence – and after spending the day riding one, it is well-founded. **CRI**

THE BIKER COMPANY'S YAMAHA XS650

The continued popularity of café racers has not only influenced private builders to create classic machinery of the style commonly seen over 50 years ago, and their hi-tech modern equivalents, but their prominence in the world of motorcycling in general has brought a recognition from those who wish to promote their businesses. With a change in business name, The Biker Company in Gloucestershire, England (www.thebikercompany.com) wanted a bike that would show its commitment to the cause, that it could use as a promotional device and as shop décor, as well as being something that would be great fun to ride. And this exceptional Yamaha XS650 is the result, with a style that epitomises the breed, and a circular reference to the company in question! – *Dave Manning* CRI

...at Cadwell Park on a track day

QUEEN OF SPEED

BIKE INSTRUCTOR NATASHA SWABY TALKS FAMILY, R1s, TRACK DAYS, R1s, MAINTENANCE, R1s, REBUILDS, R1s, BLOOD BIKES AND... YUP... R1s

INTERVIEW: MICHAEL COWTON

"I WOULD ALWAYS BE IN THE SHED WHEN DAD WAS SERVICING HIS BIKES; THE ONE HOLDING A TORCH AND TOOLS, AND CONSTANTLY ASKING QUESTIONS"

Dad Nigel and Tasha at the Isle of Man TT

Natasha Swaby blames her love of bikes, and specifically R1s, on her dad Nigel. Well, if someone has got to take responsibility, it might as well be a parent, eh? That is not to say others shall remain blameless. Her grandfather rode, and so, too, did her late uncle, Max Cheetham.

From the age of nine, Tasha would ride pillion with her father. Often, he found himself having to sneak out of the house with his gear on and ride off, conscious that his daughter was always prepared for her next ride.

A Yamaha man through and through, R1s remain Nigel's passion. The iconic 1000cc sports bike was first released in 1998 and has since gone through numerous iterations. Tasha's payment for riding pillion was to clean the rear wheel, so out would come the box of baby wipes and cleaning products. A chore to some, she loved every aspect of it, and a passion for two wheels was born. "I would always be in the shed when dad was servicing his bikes; the one holding a torch and tools, and constantly asking questions. I loved my time with him, and still do," she says.

Two wheels were to turn to four when her dad insisted that his daughter start driving and get her test under her belt before any more talk about bikes. Like all good daughters, she did as she was told, only to return to her passion two years later. "Out of the blue I thought, right, I am going to go for it; pass my bike test and do it as a surprise for dad, but he knew all along what I was doing, and commented: 'What took you so long!'"

Tasha had taken her test on a Suzuki Gladius with The Bike Academy in Lincoln, all the while continuing her obsession with mechanics. While Nigel had enjoyed working his way through various model of bikes, including a 1998 red, white and black R1, a blue GSXR 1000 and a blue 2009 R1, Tasha would spend the winter months with Uncle Max stripping and cleaning his diverse collection of bikes as well as her own bike, preparing them ready for the next season.

The first bike she owned was a Suzuki GSXR Slingshot 750. Nigel had purchased it with the intention of doing it up, but Tasha had grown impatient and decided that was to become her first bike. As she recalls: "The bike was not a pretty picture, but she was rideable. As soon as I passed my test, I decided to ride to a local village via the back roads. Upon arrival the heavens opened, and I got soaked!"

After a year enjoying the Slingshot, she had decided on something more modern; faster. That was to be a 2004 R1 and her first 'big bike'. After only a year her thoughts then turned to a track bike. Uncle Max came up with a suggestion. "I'll buy the Slingshot off you, restore it to showroom condition, and you can buy it back for the price of the restoration." Max had a passion for finding and restoring bikes, mostly Suzukis, from Slingshots to Slabsides. At the time of his death in June 2021, he had amassed a stunning collection of 25 bikes, many of which were to be passed down through family and friends.

When the time for her first track day arrived, Tasha decided on her 2004 R1 road bike. She went with Max on a particularly cold February day, and ended up sliding off, causing less damage to the bike than her pride. "That first track day was quite scary," she recalls. "I had been riding the Slingshot for a year and then the R1 for a further year, so I was not massively confident on the road at that point. However, further track days began to bring out the confidence in my riding.

"Track days are beneficial for me because I quite like to ride fast. It gives me such a good feeling and improves my riding no end. I am not interested in lap times, and simply want to improve my riding technique."

Having had in her possession Nigel's Slingshot already, Tasha's attention then turned to her dad's 2013 R1. Having enjoyed a ride-out to a local bikers' stop, they decided to swap bikes for the return journey. "I followed, having told him to go steady. I then decided to overtake him and while he was not impressed, he did admit to finding it funny." The conclusion to that scenario was that Tasha liked the bike so much, her dad never got it back! Her 2004 R1 was sold and the 2013 R1 paid for, which Nigel then used the money to buy yet another bike. That was to be a 2015 R1 which he purchased in 2016 just before he, Tasha, Max and cousin Tom travelled to the Isle of Man.

Tasha had had the 2013 R1 for a year when the itch started once again. At Webbs Motorcycles in Lincoln she had seen a magnificent Yamaha YZF-R1 60th Anniversary Edition in yellow. It had been on display by the counter for a year. Naturally, she fell in love with it. Nigel suggested she inquire about it, and as it transpired, she could afford to purchase it. So she did just that, and the 2017-registered beauty has developed into a long-standing relationship for her.

In the meantime, Nigel had switched the notch up to another level when he decided to look at the YZF-R1M. Built specifically for supreme performance on the racetrack, it was the most advanced production bike ever created by Yamaha. After much thought he decided that it was not for him and bought a brand-new 2020 R1 instead, and has since been tempting Tasha to buy one, but she is ignoring him… for now!

So how does mum Karen feel about her daughter riding particularly fast sports bikes? For most it would be a mother's worst nightmare, and particularly so in Karen's case as her brother Stephen was killed when hit by a drink driver. "Mum says if anything happens to me it will be dad's fault! While she is

not a major fan of bikes, she understands the passion for it. She has never tried to stop me, but then we never talk about bikes or speed in front of her." That is probably a good job, as on one occasion Tasha, riding her father's brand-new 2020 R1, reached 189mph. What happened to 190, then? "I was aiming for that," she says, a tad deflated.

With a current full-time role in agriculture as an assistant laboratory manager where the quality of seed and grain is conducted, plus the management of crop inspections, it is hard to imagine how Tasha manages to maintain her passion for bikes, but she does, and more. A little over four years after having passed her test she began working weekends as a part-time instructor at The Bike Academy. It was not long after she had started that the business was dissolved, to quickly re-emerge as Walt's Motorcycle Training, where she continued instructing, juggling weekends at Walt's alongside Rev 'N' Ride in Grimsby. Eventually, she decided to spend all weekends at Rev 'N' Ride, where she has remained a bike instructor for the past five years. She has since also become a valued member of LEBBS (Lincolnshire Emergency Blood Bikes Service). "The work they do is fantastic. You must have passed an advanced rider course before you can legally ride their bikes, although what many people do not realise is that you can volunteer as a car driver whilst you undergo your IAM training."

It is funny how fate often plays a hand in life. Al Lui of Lincs Repair is recognised throughout the country as the go-to man for motorcycle leather product repairs and alterations (see Volume #1 of CRI for a full feature). Nigel knew Al, having taken his new one-piece leathers for alteration, when Tasha tagged along.

The next time Tasha and Al met, Tasha had some RST leathers of her own which required work, as she explains: "It is hard to get women's leathers that are comfortable, that are a good fit, and are reasonably priced. I have to buy men's one-piece leathers because I am quite tall, but then there is never enough space in the bust area. Al inserted two panels in the required areas, and the difference was amazing. I am still wearing those same leathers to this day. Of course, there are leathers made specifically for female riders, but there are nowhere near the variation that men enjoy. They tend to be quite hard to find, and when you do find them, they are often extortionately priced."

Al has quite a number of female riders asking for leather alterations, and admits that it would be good to have a female worker with the required knowledge to deal directly with the ladies. Step forward Tasha! She is currently learning the trade and eventually hopes to join the family business full-time. "I am quite a crafty, hands-on person, and I love what I have learnt so far." Time in the workshop should work out well for her, as she and Al officially became a couple in the New Year of 2022.

Currently with five bikes under her belt, some pristine, others in a stage of undress, including an R1 which she intends to eventually use as a winter bike, it is difficult not to imagine this popular bike instructor sleeping with a tool roll as a pillow. **CRI**

"TRACK DAYS ARE BENEFICIAL FOR ME BECAUSE I QUITE LIKE TO RIDE FAST. IT GIVES ME SUCH A GOOD FEELING AND IMPROVES MY RIDING NO END"

Uncle Max enjoying a laugh with Tasha at Cadwell while watching BSB

IMAGES: INDIAN MOTORCYCLE

SCOUT ROGUE

NEW KID ON THE BLOCK

INDIAN MOTORCYCLE HAS UNLEASHED THE MOST AGGRESSIVE ITERATION OF ITS ICONIC INDIAN SCOUT WITH THE LAUNCH OF THE NEW SCOUT ROGUE

THE BIKE IS PACKED WITH ATTITUDE AND EDGE, THANKS TO ITS AGGRESSIVE STYLING AND PERFORMANCE-MINDED FEATURES

Scout Rogue

Combining iconic design with contemporary style, the Indian Scout Rogue demands attention and inspires riders to express a bolder sense of self-expression. A line-up of new features give the bike its edgy, hard-riding demeanour, including a quarter fairing, mini ape-hanger handlebars, sport-style seat, blacked-out fenders and valve covers, plus a 19-inch front wheel. The proven powertrain packs a serious punch with loads of low-end torque for snappy acceleration.

Here's Aaron Jax, Indian Motorcycle Vice President: "For so many motorcyclists, riding carries a rogue spirit – a bold statement of freedom and individuality that brings riders together – and the Scout Rogue delivers that in spades. It's an attitude that can only be found on a motorcycle, and it creates a totally unique level of camaraderie and community, and that's what the Scout Rogue is all about."

So, if you're looking for a bike that stands out from the crowd, then this could well be it. The Scout Rogue inspires rider confidence with a low seat height and manageable wheelbase, while a low centre of gravity provides superior handling for all riders – regardless of experience and skill level.

Riders looking to personalise their ride can do so through countless Indian Motorcycle accessories that enhance the bike's performance, style and comfort. You can achieve a smoother, more comfortable ride with increased suspension travel from adjustable piggyback rear shocks. Using twist knobs, riders can easily dial-in their compression and rebound damping settings.

For extra custom-inspired styling and additional performance information, it is possible to add an auxiliary tachometer with shift light. Mounting next to the standard instrumentation, the accessory keeps the rider aware of the engine's rpm and enhances the bike's high-performance style. An LED shift light illuminates to indicate recommended shift points.

Whether riding solo or two-up, exploring a town or crushing miles, Indian Motorcycle offers a host of comfort and touring accessories. Scout Rogue riders can personalise their ergonomics with the Rider Comfort Seat, not forgetting the Syndicate two-up seat and Syndicate low profile passenger backrest for added comfort for passengers. If packing gear, add the black saddlebag, solo luggage rack, and a black, water-resistant solo rack bag.

In addition, the Scout Rogue's stock quarter fairing and sport-style solo seat are now available as added accessories for Scout and Scout Bobber models. The Indian Motorcycle quarter fairing delivers custom style in a high-profile location at the front of the bike. The fairing encircles the headlight and creates a look that is both classic and sporty. The quarter fairing can be colour-matched for Scout Rogue models, Scout models from

2015-2022, and Scout Bobber models from 2018-2022.

The sport-style Syndicate solo seat provides long-riding comfort, as an upraised rear lip creates a comfortable bucket that keeps riders planted during hard acceleration. The interior padding provides an ideal blend of comfort and support, and the black, leather-like vinyl seat covering provides long-term, all-weather durability. The Syndicate solo seat also fits Scout Bobber models from 2018-2022.

The bike itself delivers 70kW (94hp) by way of a liquid-cooled, 1133cc (69 cubic-inch) V-Twin motor and is available in an attractive sagebrush smoke, black smoke midnight and stealth grey. For new riders, the Scout Rogue will also be available in A2 compliant specification.

Complementing the Scout Rogue is the Indian Motorcycle Rogue clothing and gear collection, which personifies blacked-out styling and has been designed for men and women looking for simple, clean lines with tones of black and grey. **CRI**

Images show the North American model and may have accessories fitted. International models may vary.

MEDAZA
KUBO

This truly unique build by Mick O'Shea and Don Cronin of Medaza Cycles in Cork, Ireland, shows that the café racer idiom extends far, far further than cramming a Triumph twin into a Norton frame. While the idea stemmed from using the spare parts that lay in storage – a Honda Cub 50 and a pair of MZ wheels – the reality is that every single part of this amazing creation has been caressed and fettled into the perfect form through Don and Mick's collective talents. With an engine capacity three times that of when it left the factory, and uprated brakes and suspension, Kubo fits the definition of a café racer being modified for performance gains, and looks damned fine, too. – *Dave Manning* CRI

STYLE COUNCIL

ADD A TOUCH OF CLASS TO YOUR RIDES ALONG THE HIGHWAYS, BYWAYS AND BOULEVARDS WITH MICHAEL COWTON'S SELECTION OF SOME OF THE LATEST GEAR. GO ON, YOU KNOW YOU CAN'T RESIST…

GARMIN ZUMO XT

£429.99 | GARMIN.COM

How often have you been enjoying your smartphone navigation app to guide you to your destination, and the battery has failed at the precise moment when you least expect it? Stranded and frustrated, it has probably happened to many of us at one time or another… including me! I have been fortunate of late to be handed the keys to a new Honda Rebel 1100 CMX on long-term loan. With the intention of covering reviews of country inns around the UK and Europe, a dedicated GPS seemed the best way forward. Garmin has an excellent reputation in this field, and as a result I managed to get hold of the latest Zumo XT unit.

It boasts an ultra-bright, 5.5 inch all-terrain motorcycle navigator built for adventure. The sat-nav comes pre-loaded with on-road and off-road maps across Europe and there is no subscription required, so that's a bonus. It also includes turn-by-turn directions with an option to switch between on-road maps, topographic maps and BirdsEye satellite imagery with direct-to-device downloads. No need to worry about approaching hazards and the weather, as you will receive regular hazard alerts alongside live traffic and weather updates.

It gets better. The 1280x720p HD resolution display is glove-friendly and rain-resistant. From a safety aspect, included is Bluetooth hands-free calling, automatic incident notifications, and pairing with a compatible inReach satellite communicator (sold separately).

I was discussing the unit with a fellow biker who was after a new sat-nav, and liked to be able to record his routes. I told him it was possible with the Zumo XT by using the track recorder, which he could then save and/or share for future trips. Inside the box you will find a set of instructions; a rubberised ball-mount system which is compatible with RAM; electrical power cable; mini-USB cable; and automotive suction cup mount and power cable. The only items I purchased separately were a traditional RAM handlebar mounting kit, a protective cover for the mounting bracket, and a carry-case for the unit. The included mount allows the user to hardwire the unit to the bike's electrical system. I did seek help for hardwiring the unit for constant power, and for that I popped along to my local bike mechanic for his wiring wizardry. From the mounting bracket on the handlebar, Carl fed the cable under the tank and wired it directly to the battery (the parts include a crimp-style ring terminal for connecting the wiring harness directly to the terminal). With a continuous powered solution, it was then simply a case of pushing in the power supply button to activate the device.

As a robust navigation unit with a superb, easily visible screen, I have no doubt the Zumo XT's basic functions will become fairly intuitive, and with so many more features to be enjoyed over and above what I have mentioned here, will ultimately prove to be the future perfect go-to travelling companion. **CRI**

KNOX HAND ARMOUR ORSA OR3 TEXTILE GLOVE

£99.99 | PLANET-KNOX.COM

I first came across the innovative BOA fit system on a pair of the uniquely styled Knox Handroid Pod gloves. Dialling in the system on the back of the glove is simplicity itself: push in the dial to engage, turn clockwise and note the clicking ratchet system which dials in the lace which closes the cuff for a precision fit, and pull up for fast release. Simples.

I am not sure where the name BOA came from, but it wouldn't surprise me if it is related to the boa constrictor, notorious for its deadly grip, but then you ain't gonna die from suffocation or by the obstruction of blood flow (unless you buy the wrong fit!) with the new ORSA OR3 textile glove. The gloves are comfortable, lightweight and abrasion resistant, soft and flexible, and perfect for spring/summer wear. They are manufactured in a short length, and boast a perforated leather palm combined with highly breathable textile, so ventilation is no issue. A honeycomb gel layer is in place in the knuckle region and along the fingers, offering a high standard of protection against any impact injuries to the hand, while additional protection against abrasion comes from finger sliders. You are also treated to Knox's Scaphoid Protection System, which refers to the sliders located on the palm area of the glove, specifically engineered to safeguard riders against breaking the scaphoid bone in case of an accident, that being one of the most commonly broken bones in accidents. **CRI**

OXFORD ORIGINAL APPROVED DENIM JEANS

£119.99 | OXFORDPRODUCTS.COM

If first impressions are anything to go by, then Oxford has come up trumps. No doubt like many a biker, we all love a nice pair of jeans that can be worn both on and off the bike; jeans that offer comfort and safety, but are not too bulky to look out of place down the local.

In the past, some jeans I have worn have either been too slim for my taste, ride up, or are low-slung, hipster style, which I never like. Not so the straight fit, two-year aged jeans we have here. For the techies, they are constructed from triple stitched Armourlite 13.5oz denim interwoven with high tenacity polyamide yarn and CE armour.

For the non techies, if you are looking for a pair of nice-fitting jeans with a high waist and a wide enough hem to comfortably go over a pair of boots, oh, and at a keen price point, too, then look no further.

Armourlite is a durable denim that maintains a vintage look and softness, with two-way stretch added to aid comfort. These jeans are impregnated with quick-dry technology which helps draw perspiration and increases water repellency. Included is CE level 2 flexible knee and CE level 1 flexible hip armour, and features include belts loops, and a traditional five-pocket jean design.

I thought at first the knee pads were a tad wide and bulky, but they soon bedded in. A purchase of a set of breathable, flexible armoured base layers with CE knee, hip and coccyx armour, offers the option of removing the armour from the jeans if I wish. **CRI**

SENA OUTRUSH R BLUETOOTH HELMET

£249.99 | SENA.COM

I am a fan of Sena comms units and have also enjoyed wearing the various helmets Sena offers. The new Outrush flip-front helmet has been made for complete wireless connectivity on the move, without the fad of having to fit cables, microphones, speakers or intercom units.

The premium, dual homologated modular helmet enjoys Sena's latest mobile communications technology, allowing the wearer to pair it with a smartphone for turn-by-turn GPS directions. You can also ride along while listening to your favourite musical tunes; dial into FM radio; receive phone calls; or even communicate with up to four other riders. For group chats, you can expect up to a half-mile range, and battery life comes in at an impressive 12 hours.

Advanced noise control filters cut out much of the road and wind noise, while audio multitasking lessens the volume of music or GPS directions when someone speaks.

Although comfortable and enjoying the versatility of the flip-front style, I found the helmet a tad on the heavy side, but that's only a minor point. With all the tech pre-installed and ready to use straight from the box, the Outrush R is available in two colour options, matte black or glossy white, in sizes S-XXL. **CRI**

OXFORD HARDY BOOT

£119.99 | OXFORDPRODUCTS.COM

Whether you are out for a pleasant, leisurely ride in the countryside, or on a long journey, it is clearly important to wear a casual, but comfortable, riding boot. That goes without saying.

Ah, but just think about the weather, which we all do in the UK. Are you going to get caught out in a sudden downpour? If so, will your boots withstand the rain? No? Then it's time to take action. No need to go mad. I'm not an adventure biker, so I always go for something more casual, yet still durable, such as the new leather-constructed Hardy Waterproof Urban Motorcycle Boots from Oxford Products, which feature a waterproof and breathable Dry2Dry membrane. The styling may sit in the vintage category, but the boots are packed with modern-day convenience and features, including triple needle stitching, and a reinforced heel and a shank reinforced sole. Comfortable straight from the box, they are available in either brown or charcoal, in sizes UK 6.5 (EU 40) to UK 13 (EU 47). **CRI**

Kit

KEIS HEATED VEST V106 & HEATED 'SHORTY' BONDED-TEXTILE GLOVES

VEST £125 | GLOVES £190 | KEISAPPAREL.COM

Power to the people, that's what I say in a warm-hearted way. Now come on, how many of you have returned home from a ride these past few months only to find your hands and fingers in some sort of paralysed, semi-frozen state? I know I have.

Winter gloves are fine, but heated gloves take things to an extra level. No one wants to experience the frigid cold as it only makes us miserable before we even press the start button. There is nothing worse than bulking up in a layering system either, because it doesn't make for either a comfortable or pleasurable ride. So, how best to deliver the warmth? I turned to Keis for the answer.

It manufactures a range of heated clothing, from jackets to puffers to vests to gloves to bottoms. Keis' Heated Vest V106 is very much a dual-purpose garment, meaning that you can use it either via a battery pack and charger, or by powering it to your bike's 12V battery via a supplied vehicle power supply lead. Strategically positioned heat panels on the chest and down the back take care of the magic in the breathable, lightweight, softshell fabric. The vest includes dedicated zipped pockets for cables and the power controller, which has three settings, depending on how much heat you require. The leads can be neatly

stored away while riding. Such was the heat level, that it wasn't long before I switched from High to Medium. Impressive indeed. Current draw is 1.3A, and typical power 15.6W. The wonderful thing about the vest is that it can be worn off the bike, too, over a base layer, as it looks plenty stylish and therefore boasts a multitude of uses. The V106 bodywarmer is also available as the V501 and V501 Premium Heated Vest in red and black colourway (as pictured).

So, what about those hands, then? Keis has again come up trumps with the new Bonded-Textile Heated Gloves. The original G701 gloves now have a shorter, streamline cuff, without battery pockets. Called the G701S Shorty Gloves, you need not worry if your jacket has reasonably tight-fitting cuffs because the Shorty will fit comfortably underneath. You can easily link the gloves to a Keis heated vest via a connecting

power lead or once again power them from a motorcycle battery power lead. The gloves have a Ballistic Spandex outer shell with a semi bonded Hipora waterproof and breathable membrane, offering the rider excellent comfort and performance no matter what the conditions. The palm is made from a high-quality synthetic leather, providing the benefits of a fine leather look, but with better production features. They also feature 3M Thinsulate insulation, designed specifically for biking in cold weather, and are fully certified to the new EU PPE Regulation 13594:2015. A micro carbon fibre heating panel sits across the back of the hands and over the top of the fingers. **CRI**

TUCANO URBANO EL'TOP HELMET

£119.99 | TUCANOURBANO.COM

I've said this before, and am happy to repeat myself – you don't have to pay the earth for a good-quality helmet, and the EL'TOP is a case in point. For starters, I like the look of this rather trendy polycarbonate demi–jet helmet, which comes with a sun visor and Dynamic Flow ventilation. Essentially, this is a great, fully optimal helmet for those fresh summer days, thanks to the ventilation system, and when you want to keep your head warm, you have the benefit of the aeration covers. With the double visor addressing the needs of every season and time of day, we have

both form and functionality. With an ECE 22.05 approval rating, the helmet is constructed of a thermoplastic polycarbonate shell, with the inner in high impact absorption, dual-density EPS.

The perforations have metal mesh inserts, with anti–irritant microfibre under chin fastener and Quick Release System. The polycarbonate anti–scratch treatment transparent visor is Class A approved, and the visor cover is made of scratchproof silicone. With ample space around the ears, it is possible to fit the Tucano Urbano Bluetu intercom kit (302BTC) with integrated pads, which can be purchased separately at a smidgeon over £80, and allows you to make/receive calls and listen to music in wireless mode.

With detachable and washable cheek pads, and the removable, breathable, hypoallergenic microfibre lining, with maxi Aero 3D mesh inserts also removable and washable, you can stay fresh all-day long. In various colours, XS-XL. Vent covers are available at £8.99 for the black or £12.99 for coloured options. **CRI**

RECEKA BASE LAYER

£19.99 | RECEKA.CO.UK

Sometimes you have to dig deep for what you really yearn for. I have a few base layers lying around, but none with a high enough neckline to suit my needs. Then, every once in a while, a new base layer comes along, one that is worth investigating, particularly when one bears in the mind the cost.

Can this be true? A suitable base layer that costs under £20? Time to try. Receka is a new name to me, but deserves recognition for what has proved to be its excellent long sleeve base layer, manufactured from a supportive lycra fleece fabric. According to Receka, the top was originally designed to be worn under one- and two-piece leathers, but has since caught on with those involved in other sporting activities, including hiking, which is where I came in all those years ago. In essence, the lycra fleece fibres on the rear of the fabric create an air pocket so warm air can be trapped between the skin and fabric, keeping the wearer warmer. Conversely, in warmer weather, moisture is transported from the surface of the skin via the raised lycra fibres to the outer section of the fabric, which then evaporates when in contact with air, helping the wearer stay cooler. When Receka contacted me, I opted for an XL, which normally comes up like a second skin, well, really tight – I could term it an 'athletic fit' – but it helps my figure. It was suggested that I go up to a 2XL, just to be safe.

I'm glad I did, as the fit is perfect. The top has a really nice high collar; the material is lightweight and soft, and hopefully will prove to be durable, making it perfect for all-day rides throughout the seasons. I opted for some particularly chilly days to check out the base layer. Well layered up, including a new Zeis heated vest, not once did I feel a chill through my leather jacket, and peeling off the layers once back home, I kept the Receka on around the house, washing the bike, and packing things away. Impressive indeed. Do not be put off by the word 'lycra'. This is not a 100% lycra top, but a fleece fabric variant, guaranteeing warmth when you need it most. The base layer weighs in at a mere 0.5kg, and sizing is medium (38-40in/96-102cm), large (40-42in102-107cm), XL (44-46in/107-117cm) and XXL (46-48in/117-122cm). **CRI**

HOTPANTS FROM KEIS

£165 | KEISAPPAREL.COM

It's time to ditch those itchy, bulky underlayers and keep legs cosy, even on the chilliest rides, with the new T103RP Heated Trousers from Keis. We reckon they are ideal for riders of café racers, which, as we know, offer little protection for the legs.

Designed to be worn under riding trousers, they are made from a lightweight, breathable Softshell fabric with an elasticated waist, so they fit comfortably without restricting movement. When the temperature drops, strategically positioned heated panels with micro alloy element technology provide instant warmth, eliminating the feeling that legs won't work when stopping at junctions or for fuel, etc. A connection flap is built in for adding a Standard or Bluetooth Keis Power Controller (optional extras), enabling the user to change the heat setting, and to switch on and off. Power for the T103RP can come directly from the bike's 12V battery via the power lead supplied, or they can be connected to a Keis heated jacket, bodywarmer or vest, for all-over warmth. The current draw is a modest 3.25A and typical power is a substantial 39W.

Available in sizes XS-3XL (UK 32in-44in waist), they come with all required wiring and easy-to-follow instructions. **CRI**

WEISE LAYERS

£34.99 (FOR THE PAIR) | WEISECLOTHING.COM

Weise has added two new base layer options to its range, helping riders stay comfortable through all four seasons: an insulated thermal top and pants for the colder months and a lightweight set for spring and summer. Designed for the colder months, the thermal top and pants have a luxurious fleece lining to help insulate, while still retaining breathability. The soft-touch fabric has flat-finished seams, so it won't rub and chafe, and has a light stretch for mobility on and off the bike. Both are available in sizes S-3XL. £34.99 for the top and £34.99 for the pants.

The base layer set comprises a long sleeve top and trousers, both of which offer excellent moisture management and have light insulation to keep the wearer comfy from late spring through to early autumn. They are made from a soft, flexible, and light-stretch fabric, with flat-finished seams for comfort. Thinner than the winter versions, they sit comfortably under close-fitting leather suits and tighter summer kit. The Weise base layer set comes in sizes S- 2XL. **CRI**

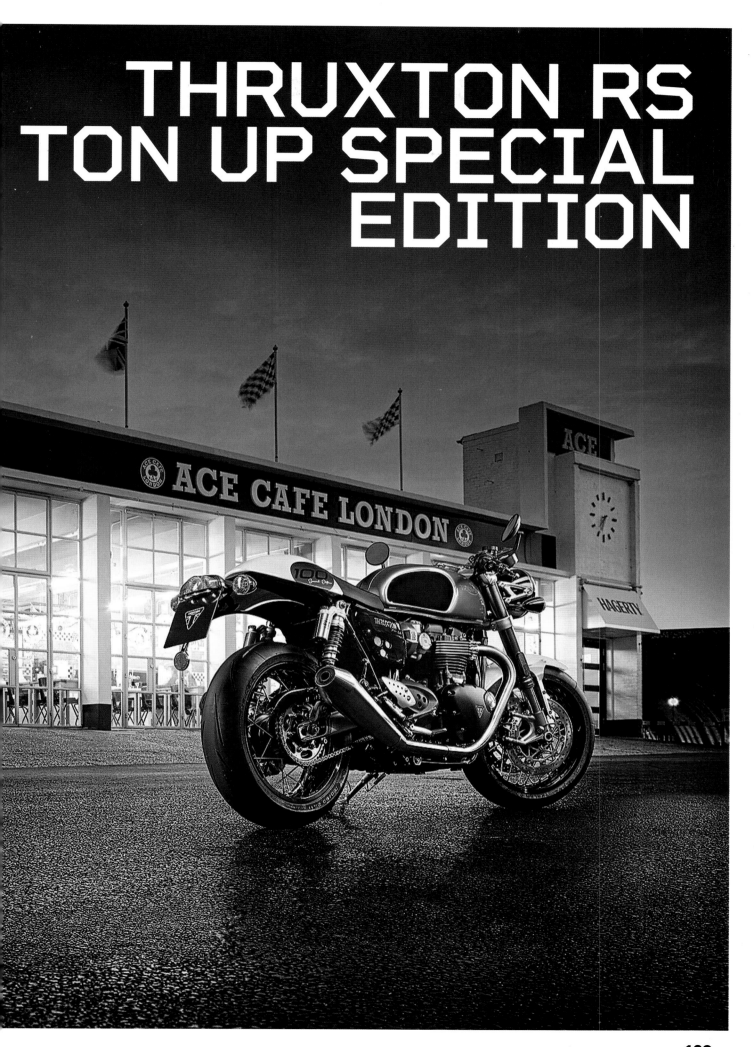

THRUXTON RS TON UP SPECIAL EDITION